MoonWind at Large

Books by Constant Waterman

The Journals of Constant Waterman:
Paddling, Poling, and Sailing for the Love of It

MoonWind *at Large: Sailing Hither and Yon*

Landmarks You Must Visit in Southeast Connecticut

Vincus the Invisible Divulges His Secret Recipe for Maple Pistachio
Birch Beer Raspberry Ripple

Vincus the Invisible Visits Planet Earth

MoonWind at Large

Sailing Hither and Yon

Written & Illustrated by
**Matthew Goldman,
aka Constant Waterman**

BREAKAWAY BOOKS
HALCOTTSVILLE, NEW YORK
2012

MoonWind at Large: Sailing Hither and Yon
Text & illustrations © 2011 by Matthew Goldman aka Constant Waterman

ISBN 978-1-891369-95-7
Library of Congress Control Number: 2012932780

Published by Breakaway Books
P.O. Box 24
Halcottsville, NY 12438
www.breakawaybooks.com

The following pieces originally appeared in these publications:

Messing About in Boats: Most of the stories included here have appeared or will appear in my regular column in *Messing About in Boats*. My sincere thanks to its publisher and founder, Bob Hicks, for his ongoing support.

Good Old Boat: Reflections on Ocean Cruising, There Was a Time.

Wind Check: The Whitehall, Dock and Dine, Independence Day.

Points East: Hamburg Cove, Verisimilitude, Warm Enough to Sail, Purchasing *MoonWind,* Hello, Hello, Hello!

Ocean Magazine: Thanksgiving 2007.

Ink Magazine: Wooden Boat Parade.

Excerpt from "Fiddler Jones" by Edgar Lee Masters.

Illustrations of Mermaid & Little Gull Light first appeared in *Points East.*

Illustration of Poseidon first appeared in *Windcheck.*

Illustration of Pawnee courtesy of Chris-Craft Boats and Sparkman and Stephens.

FIRST EDITION

Contents

For all those whose white hair
Is attributable to salt spray

Introduction

Well, it's happened again. April has slipped away, having come in with gale-force winds and now going out with scarcely breeze enough to strain my sails. Following a deluge of daffodils, the azaleas and magnolias chose to blossom. The pear trees now overflow with flowers; the ornamental cherries grow nearly too pink to look upon without some dazzle protection.

I had to go sailing just to escape the beauty of it all.

Sailing is how I justify my office at home where I write about going sailing.

It seemed a pleasant day within the breakwater, so I bent on my smaller genoa jib, a faded 115. This is a handy sail for anything from light air to upward of twenty knots, at which point *Moon Wind* tends to get a bit headstrong. Yesterday, I could have flown my larger genoa jib without any problem. I wafted about the mouth of the Thames at a leisurely two to three knots and watched the ferries come and go and kept a weather eye alert for mermaids.

With days such as these, nothing happens at all worth writing about. However, I need to compile another book or my publisher won't put any checks in the mail. This has serious consequences, as then I can't afford to feed my boat. I've become a virtual slave to this computer. My adoring public demands I write a column. My wife demands I spend more time in my office and leave her alone. The Pusslet demands I keep my *Webster's Unabridged* open to the entry titled "nap."

Ah, the unfairness of it all. I've scarcely time to go boating.

Moon Wind, of course, has her own demands to make. She's such an adventurous lass that I'm forced to keep her tethered with extra lines, else she'd be off on errantry of her own. Yesterday was nearly calm with a tiny wind from the southeast. After I'd cast off every line, *Moon-*

Wind just lay in her slip, assuming an obviously studied nonchalance—waiting her chance to climb on that weedy rock across the
channel when I wasn't looking. I put the motor into reverse; backed
and turned and puttered out past the piers.

Four people on a forty-footer were rigging her for the season, practicing epithets on her intractable roller furling. The slips are gradually
filling up, but the process seems interminable. By the time the final
boat goes in, some folks will have considered hauling out.

"June, July, and August," one woman said to me. "That's all the
sailing I care about. Who wants to be on the sea when it's rough and
cold?"

Well, yesterday, ashore, it was sixty degrees. On the water, it was
probably closer to fifty. With the windchill, I was glad I'd worn my
long johns. Especially on a little boat, you don't get to move about
much, and your blood assumes the consistency of a stranded jellyfish.
But *MoonWind* generally tracks pretty well a few points off the breeze.
Then I get up and stroll about the slanting deck and find something
useful to do. When hurrying tide and hurrying wind choose to oppose
each other, to hang on constitutes something useful to do.

I wore my safety harness yesterday, but never attached the lanyard.
I've seldom drowned when the breeze blew a mere eight knots. Besides, I had my life vest on. That would serve to keep me afloat until
I could freeze to death. There's such a thing as worrying overmuch
about one's demise. I make it a point to stay limber and agile and keep
one hand on a grab rail or the lifeline. The water this time of year is
just a mite chilly. I much prefer my water hot and out of the shower-
head, thank you.

So, I didn't drown and the mermaids didn't abduct me and I was-
n't run down but a couple of times by the ferry to Orient Point. And
the sun warmed me sufficiently when I recollected the sunny side of
the sail; and the breeze from the east forced lovely fresh air into my
grateful lungs; and the world spread wide as wide before my senses.
The seagull hung in the airstream and cried of his affection for little

rock crabs, and a tug towed a barge out of the Thames and set a course for the glamorous Great White Way. And the only thing I knew to do was to keep on sailing my boat.

Just as you, I have a list of projects aboard that cries out for attention. But I empathize with Edgar Lee Masters's "Fiddler Jones," who finds work but a distraction.

> *The earth keeps some vibration going*
> *There in your heart, and that is you.*
> *And, if the people find you can fiddle,*
> *Why, fiddle you must, for all your life.*
> *What do you see, a harvest of clover?*
> *Or a meadow to walk through to the river?*

And I've fiddled now with all my boats the better half of a century, and walked through every meadow to any river. So now I'm hardly likely to change my ways: hardly likely to cease to play on the riverbank; hardly likely to cease to fare forth in search of consoling breezes; hardly likely to cease to ply my effusive wit to presume to tell you about it.

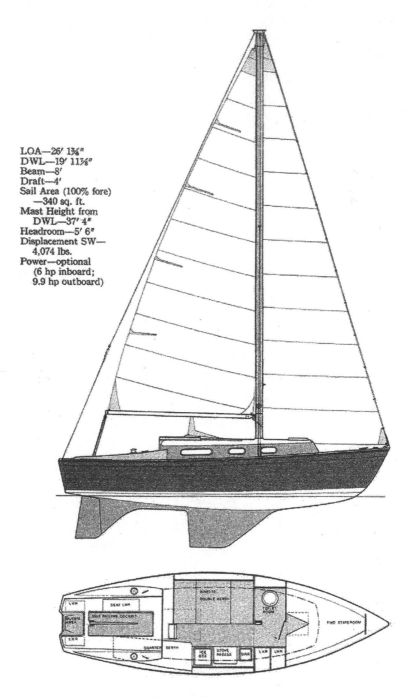

LOA—26′ 1¾″
DWL—19′ 11⅞″
Beam—8′
Draft—4′
Sail Area (100% fore)
  —340 sq. ft.
Mast Height from
  DWL—37′ 4″
Headroom—5′ 6″
Displacement SW—
  4,074 lbs.
Power—optional
  (6 hp inboard;
  9.9 hp outboard)

Chris-Craft Pawnee

Purchasing *Moon Wind*

I recollect the day I purchased *Moon Wind*.

Our marina has an area of the hard, across the road from where boats are stored for the winter, designated the graveyard. Here reside those boats that haven't been launched for a couple of years or more. Some are in arrears on storage fees, some seemingly abandoned. Owners die, or move away, or lose interest in shoving the seas apart and drenching their souls in sunshine.

Generally, when the number of boats in the boneyard approaches a dozen, the marina resolves its problem of limited space by holding an auction. About every other year, they post notices, listing those boats about to be sold off. The auction generally takes place late in September or maybe early October.

In 2003, I decided my little Cape Dory Typhoon was too small for Paula and me. I listed her on the Internet and looked for a larger vessel. I couldn't afford very much. It seemed most prudent to choose an old boat from the boneyard and make an offer. Trouble was, none of the boats coming up for auction was really what I wanted. I wanted something large enough to go coasting with some comfort, but small enough to maintain and repair myself.

The closest I found was a twenty-six-foot, twin-keeled sloop—the type they build and sail in the British Isles, especially Scotland, where the tides are fifteen to twenty feet and the boats can rest on the bottom when the avid tide runs out. A friend of mine warned me against this type of craft.

"They're stiff enough to be seaworthy," he told me, "but they don't maneuver well. And you shouldn't buy something with an outboard well—you're only asking for trouble. You can't tip the motor out of the water and, when it gets rough, water comes sloshing up into the well and interferes with your steering. You'll yaw from Fishers Island Sound all the way to Nantucket."

I've never been very good at taking advice. Too obstinate, or maybe just not too bright. The auction found me admiring this twin-keeled beauty and hoping that no one else would want to bid for her.

As the auction progressed, powerboats and sailboats were claimed by joyous buyers. Some of the boats were in such poor shape they were bought for only their engines. A couple proved so derelict that no one would bid at all. A few sparked the interest of several people and went for as much as three or four thousand dollars. That was about my limit, but I hoped to get a bargain—don't we all?

The bidding finally started on *my* sloop.

"Who'll give me two thousand dollars?" the auctioneer yelled.

The marina was so quiet I could hear a seagull sing.

"How about fifteen hundred?"

No one responded.

"A thousand?" he asked, looking straight at me. I gave him a grin.

"How about five hundred?" I said.

"Make that six," he replied.

"Seven," came a voice from behind me.

I turned around. A boy—he couldn't have been more than twenty-five—stood there with eyes alight. He wanted this boat.

"Eight," I responded.

"Nine!"

Over and back we went, urged on by the auctioneer. I felt someone jostle my elbow.

"Make that fourteen!" I bawled.

"You don't want that boat," my friend confided.

"Sixteen hundred!" I shouted.

"She's not the right boat for you."

"Eighteen hundred!" I yelled.

"I've found the boat you're looking for," he said.

"Two thousand dollars!" I hollered.

"She's right out here on a mooring," he said. "You can take her for a sail."

"Going once for twenty-one hundred dollars!" the auctioneer cried.

"She's a lovely boat," my friend persisted. "A Chris-Craft Pawnee. A Sparkman and Stephens design."

"Going twice for twenty-one hundred dollars!" the auctioneer said. He looked at me. I looked at the lad behind me, then shook my head.

"Sold for twenty-one hundred dollars to that young fellow in the back!" the auctioneer yelled, and everyone applauded.

"Come on," said my friend. "I got the keys to the yard skiff from the broker."

We puttered out to a mooring and there she lay: a dark green sloop with white deck and cabin, twenty-six feet long. A lovely old boat. She winked at me and, of course, I fell in love. She was just over thirty; experienced: the ideal age for a mistress—every man's dream. I named her *MoonWind*.

We've had an affair for eight years now, and we're comfortable together. I sleep with her at every opportunity. But you understand how these things go. Now she's past forty, I may just trade her in for a younger lover.

But please don't tell her I said so.

Poseidon—Royal Naval Dockyards, Bermuda

Reflections on Ocean Cruising

That evening I returned from the Caribbean, we buried Old Cat amid the flowers in the lee of that fieldstone wall where she was wont to wile her waning days, basking in this hot, high sun of June. God grant someone buries me on a breezy knoll amid the glad wild roses, with an unconditional prospect of the sea.

One comes to wonder, after a careful while, whence it all comes; whither it all may tend; whether there be any sense, design, or relevance in all or any of what we know as life. I only know that time is something we borrow piecemeal; that to tear off huge gobbets of it and expect to sate ourselves is mindless gluttony. I want to savor the bits, the morsels, the spangled bioluminescence left in the wake of those of you with agendas.

I have just returned from sailing some fifteen hundred nautical miles aboard a Jeanneau 37, having made a passage as straight as wind and sea might allow.

(Steer small; keep the edge of your spinnaker taut; don't extravagate past the margin of expedition; tune your weather backstay till the mast is arched to give you maximum draft. There. I think we've gained another tenth of a knot. Maybe two.)

Hour after hour. Day after day. Through crystal nights when the stars proved too, too many, and through nights of driving rain. And when our hull speed dropped to under three knots, we started the motor.

(At only half throttle, we should be able to maintain four knots and consume but a third of a gallon of diesel per hour, per hour, per hour. But remember: We have but diesel enough to take us three hundred miles.)

We made two runs of about a week: Spanish Town, Virgin Gorda to St. George's Harbor, Bermuda; thence, two days later, to Casco Bay,

Maine—just 'round Portland Head. We attempted never to have a day's run of less than a hundred miles. Our best run, our first day out, was 150. We allowed eight days to reach St. George's; we did it in seven and a half. We allowed seven days to reach Casco Bay, and made it to our mooring in six and a half. Were we efficient, concerted, productive, and copacetic, or what?

Yes—or what.

I've determined I don't care to spend my sailing by racing the clock, the wind, the tide, the season. I want to proceed in a desultory, relaxed, serendipitous fashion. Rather than spoon my cereal into my ear while bracing my leg against the leeward port light, I want to sit at a level table while anchored in some by-water; to sip my French roast, to write in my journal; to delight in the passage of earth through heaven without regretting the fourteen nautical miles I might have made good had I raised my sails with the budding light and fled the wind instead of waiting until I'd washed my dishes.

So here I perch on the cusp of maturation, keeping my body in reserve for the best that is yet to come. I have no running backstays to adjust, no spinnaker to demand untoward vigilance. I do know how to tweak my traveler, get more lift from my jib, make my morning last till the afternoon. More than this I cannot be responsible for, nor wish to be, for morning and afternoon and night are entities that need to be savored separately and garnished with that appreciation that comes of taking small bites.

I look forward to being on the water again as a waterman, not a racer; as a raconteur, not as a logger of miles; as a connoisseur of the dip and pivot of pinion, slant of sunbeam, gurgle of ebb, and decant of foam from vintage hull through the water.

To those of you who must wake at three to take the wheel, I wish you well. There is no thrill like the heaving sea streaming astern at seven knots as you lean beneath constellations in the hugeness of tropic nights. When I feel such urges I shall cast off *Moon Wind*'s pendant and follow the plunging moon past far fringed dawn.

But morning will find me anchored in some still harbor.
I shall breakfast with birds;
Heed the creak of the piling;
Savor the breeze that slept midst upland roses.

I shall watch the steeds of Helios ascend the steep, steep sky;
Embrace the day;
Remember to breathe.
Remember to breathe.
Wait the turn of the tide.

THE CONNECTICUT RIVER

HADLYME COUNTRY STORE
HADLYME, CONNECTICUT

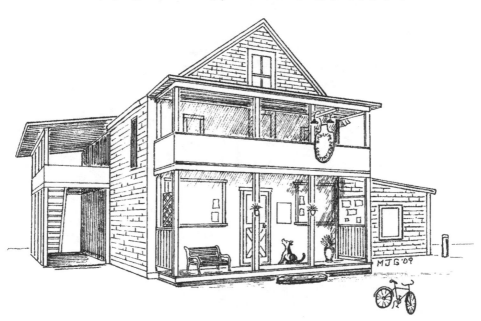

Jane's, Hamburg, Connecticut

Hamburg Cove

A lovely daybreak here in Hamburg Cove. Most of a moon last night with tier upon tier of piled purple clouds. The boaters here do their best to contribute to the quiet. Last night, some rock and roll blared from a trio of rafted cruisers. But not for long. Now, at five thirty, forty geese flock together to suggest the world wake. They noisily avenge themselves on the drowsy rock and rollers.

A great blue heron, up to her breast in ripples, stalks past the muddy shore in search of breakfast and, at whiles, ongks her approval of frogs and little fishes. A larger fish broaches beside my boat. The resultant ripples spread and spread and spread.

Many new mansions on either shore attest to progress or, at the least, to prosperity. Most of this was woods, some of it fields, when I was a boy. The mooring field I swing in now was mostly open water. Who would want to come to Hamburg Cove?

I read a book, long ago, about the Intra Coastal Waterway: the ICW. It mentioned that Hamburg Cove provides the most sheltered harbor between New York and Boston. It didn't mention how lovely it is at daybreak, with the surface of the water breathless with expectation and the birds alive to the manifest immensity of creation.

The outer cove, here in the mooring field, spreads its soft waters two hundred yards in breadth. On opposite banks, two small boathouses stand at the heads of piers. Built of vertical boards and painted barn red, they fit the rustic, arboreal landscape well. One is pristine, its pier in good repair. A yellow kayak leans against one wall.

The other I remember from decades past. It sags disastrously now— pitching forward toward the overgrown pier. Eaves high bushes shroud the double doors. The barn-red paint has faded to ocher, the shingles to mossy gray. The small side doorway gapes on a boatless gloom.

By half past six, I let go my mooring and tiptoe out the ample channel beneath the wooded hill. As always, the breeze is whimsical on the river. It comes and goes, shifts a point, ruffles my hair, then dances away and leaves my boat to drift. *MoonWind* takes it upon herself gently to jibe and descend the tranquil river wing and wing. This leaves her dreamy memoirist free to keep the entire world in perspective.

The tide has just begun to ebb; even without a breeze I shall reach the sea. Occasionally, the boom comes amidships inquisitively to inquire of her blocking. I give her direction and concentrate on the beauty all about me. Ospreys nest on every steel beacon along the river. On a small dead tree a pair of eagles roosts.

The lower river has many woods and marshes and grassy islands where loosestrife and mallows bloom amid the rushes. The eastern bank remains more rural; the western bank sprouts villages and landings. The waterfront has awoken. Fishermen are on their way to the sound. Shapely white steeples poke above ancient trees. Mooring fields teem with crops of yachts.

I come to the highway bridge, its thunderous commotion far above me. Ahead, the steel bascule bridge has closed. At my knot and a half, the train will have passed and the bridge reopened long before I arrive.

The mouth of the river spreads wide to greet Long Island Sound, but the only safe water flows between the jetties. As I pass the first lighthouse at Lynde Point, the wind picks up, although from a different quarter. Now I flatten my straining sails as I draw abeam the Breakwater Light—the lighthouse at the terminus of the jetty. Above the jittering mile of Long Sand Shoal, hundreds of terns swirl and feed and cry.

I set a course for the big red bell beyond the shoal as *MoonWind* leans to the sea.

HADLYME PUBLIC HALL
1911 ~ 2011

River Burial

This is nearly as intimate as I am accustomed to be. This weekend, I sail up the Connecticut River and scatter the mingled ashes of my long-deceased mother and father upon its waters.

My parents died over fifteen years ago. Our family owns an unused plot in Cove Cemetery, overlooking lovely Whalebone Cove. Although my parents dwelt in Hadlyme half a century, they were never really a part of the community. My father was politically active in East Haddam, but tiny, rural Hadlyme is centered in Lyme. Though the village spans two townships, only the little church is in East Haddam. That, and one of the one-room schools, the North School. Both were within the view of our home when the leaves were off the trees.

The South School, in Lyme, is by Whalebone Cove, overlooking its confluence with stony Whalebone Creek. While the North School is used as a public hall, the South School is privately owned. When I was a boy, it housed a one-man machine shop.

My parents always had a mailbox at the post office in Hadlyme. Many locals waited for the mail to be distributed in the morning and, having bought coffee at the adjoining store, settled in for a gossip. My father was too impatient ever to do this. Besides, he hadn't the slightest interest in what the village was doing; his mind was on the doings of the world. The politics and economies of nations were worth intellectual scrutiny. The machinations of the village were beneath him; the worldviews of workingmen deemed worthless.

There were other intellectuals in the village; he welcomed the chance to argufy with any. My mother volunteered at the private library up at Goodspeed's Landing. But they both belonged to organizations beyond the scope of towns, and always chaired their committees. They entertained a few local couples but were never invited into homes in the village. My mother was cordial and house-proud; the Lenox china gleamed, the sterling tea service glistened.

Though my sister and I attended Sunday school at the Hadlyme Church, the other side of the brook, my parents were never a part of the congregation. On rare occasions, my mother attended the candlelit Christmas Eve service by herself.

Why should they care to be buried in one of the prettiest spots in Hadlyme? Neither had spent a single minute admiring Whalebone Cove when they were alive. Neither had wandered the shady graveyard, recollecting their neighbors.

The only reason they bought the plot was due to our next-door neighbor. This retired gentleman devoted his time exclusively to landscaping. In addition to having an enviable lawn and productive garden, he assumed the caretaker's duties for Cove Cemetery. As a teenager, I helped him one summer to build a retaining wall for an addition to the crowded burial ground. Besides soliciting funds for the cemetery, our neighbor convinced my father to buy a plot for the four of us in this shady, terraced addition.

I could never get to bury my parents' ashes. I always had some plausible excuse. Neither professed the least belief in any sort of hereafter. I've inherited some hefty doubts, myself. What have bones to do with spiritual things? And if they have, I'd rather broadcast them upon the waters to enjoy a limitless mingling with the world.

Today, I scatter their mortal remains upon the Connecticut River. First, a scoop at the railroad bridge spanning the mouth of the river. Then a scoop at the Baldwin Bridge just above it. How many thousands of times had each of them driven across it? Then a scoop by the long-defunct Ferry Tavern on the Old Lyme shore where we spent so many enjoyable outings together.

As I ascend, I spread some ashes at every town I pass. Always some connection with my parents comes to mind. Old Saybrook, Essex, Deep River, Chester, and Haddam up the west bank. Old Lyme, Lyme, and East Haddam up the east.

Hadlyme, between these last two towns, earns my extra attention. Here spreads the welcoming entrance to Whalebone Cove, which leads to the cemetery. Here plies the ferry that bore them so many times across the river. This road from the ferry leads past our wholesome public hall and up to Hadlyme Four Corners. Gillette's Castle, perched high above the landing, stares with stony windows across the valley. Twenty minutes' shady walk away lay our homestead, Shelter Rock Farm; its long green acres my green room of that theater where my parents upstaged each other.

Two miles north of Hadlyme, Goodspeed's Landing, a part of East Haddam, clusters by the bank: the town offices, the old hotel, the Opera House, the lumbering steel swing bridge; the peaceful Rathbun Library up the hill. I scatter a scoop of ashes in memory of this; another scoop in recollection of that.

Clearance beneath our bridge is nineteen feet. Twenty yards downstream from one massive pier, I put the helm down and come about and empty the last of their lives upon the huge back eddy that churns the gravid waters. A wisp of them will linger about the landing.

Farewell and farewell.

I collapse in the cockpit. My purposeless sails flap. The ignorant wheels of hurrying cars ring on the steel decking overhead.

I idle slowly down my beautiful river. Hamburg Cove, where I hoped to spend the night, has so filled with boats, a procession of disappointed vessels motors from its mouth. I pick up a mooring in hospitable North Cove by the river mouth, and settle in with my memories.

It must be the wide-eyed harvest moon that keeps me awake tonight.

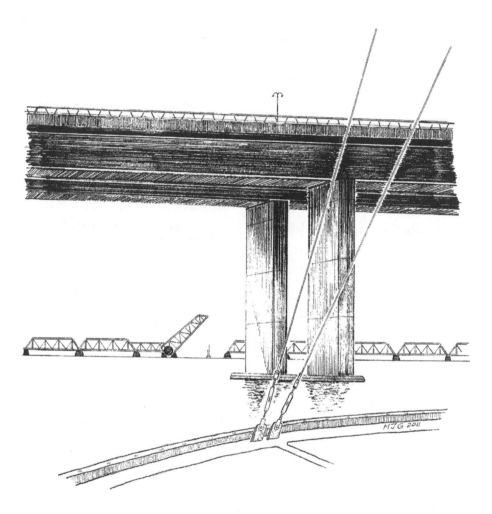

Baldwin Bridge and Old Lyme Drawbridge, Connecticut River

Dock and Dine

Yesterday I headed for the Connecticut River aboard *Moon Wind* for my annual pilgrimage to the land of my misspent youth. Everyone told me as a boy to keep away from water and little boats. I could have pursued a normal life; in which case I'd now have a normal job and a normal spouse and fourteen normal children and spend my Saturdays mowing the carpet and my Sundays refolding the literary supplement and waiting my turn for the comics.

Instead, this Sunday morning finds me on a transient mooring in a lovely sheltered cove by the mouth of the river with the low sun warming my back and some thick dark French roast amply warming the rest of me. The propane stove condescended not to burn down the galley this week, so the auspices for a pleasant morning are favorable.

The sailing yesterday proved less than auspicious. I needed to make some sixteen miles against the tide and into a westerly's eye. If I'd left at eight in the morning instead of noon, I could have saved bucking the tide, but then the wind would have raised a worse chop than it did. The first two miles took merely most of an hour. Then I needed to tack at nearly right angles to my course and found my set and drift negated my progress.

Someone of a thoughtful nature provided me with a motor. The rest of Saturday afternoon I motored against the weather, my sails secured. Between the mouth of the Thames and the Race, the chop was less than amusing. I never did don foul-weather gear, but my hair unaccountably grew rather stiff by the time I'd slopped my way past Bartlett's Reef. After that the sea smoothed out and behaved itself and the tide relented and the summer sun kindly dried what's left of my hair.

I made the turn at bell number 8 and headed for the jetty light at the mouth of the Connecticut. Only six hours to traverse the sixteen miles. With the wind now abeam, I raised my genny and throttled back my motor. I called the first mate, who was snug at home among her cats and her flowers. We agreed to meet at Saybrook Point and have dinner at the Dock and Dine.

A mile up the river, I dropped my genny and puttered up to the pier. Not many people still opted to dock on their way to dine, it seemed. The restaurant's pier, though still rugged, showed its age. The pilings had no fenders down their fronts. Another boat embraced the single ladder.

I motored to the posh marina two hundred yards downstream. Their sturdy new pier—rugged enough to drive a large vehicle over— fronts the mile-wide river for a thousand feet. Finger piers for sixty-footers sprout in every direction. The fuel pier is a hundred yards in length. The two-story dockmaster's office is furnished with computers and air-conditioning. Behind the pier lies a basin for more boats.

I pulled alongside the uttermost end of the pier—beyond the pump-out station. It was dead low tide, and the rubbing strips on the huge new pilings stopped a yard from the water—about three inches above little *MoonWind*'s rail. Apparently no one expected to service a vessel as tiny as mine. Nonetheless, two smart lads in marina jerseys ran up to handle my lines.

My stern line proved a bit short for taking a clove hitch on the piling, six feet above me. I tossed the lad another short length of line.

"How should I knot them together?" the boy inquired.

"Far be it from me to supervise an old salt like yourself," I replied. Around the mouth of this river, most boys his age have a twenty-foot boat of their own. I scrambled up to the pier as they made me fast.

"Can I leave her here for an hour while I get some supper?" I asked.

"You'll need to talk to the dockmaster," said the boys as they departed.

My forward line was secured by half a clove hitch. My stern line boasted a clove with two extra wraps for good measure, but the knot securing the two lengths of line would not have kept your lamb secured to your bedpost long enough for you to don your pajamas.

I squared things away and sought out the venerable dockmaster. He named a price for me to borrow twenty-six feet of the unused end of his pier for almost an hour. He must have misunderstood me; I hadn't intended to purchase his marina.

I motored back to the Dock and Dine and made fast with three lengths of line. As this was a no-wake zone and the breeze kept me off the pier, I refrained from disturbing the superannuated algae taking a well-earned retirement on their pilings.

The first mate arrived with breakfast fixings and bedding to stow aboard. At a little table in the restaurant's bar we launched an assault on a luscious salad, delicate crab cakes, perfectly crisp calamari.

After supper we motored to nearby North Cove. We picked up a transient mooring and settled in for a most delightful evening. The piled sky was heavily layered with purple below, then indigo, then a pale blue above. Following a stately sunset, every village about held a fireworks show. The nearest of these, a mile away at Fenwick Point, went on for nearly an hour. The grand finale came with a rousing crescendo. The smoke from the battlefield drifted out to sea.

As the minions of the night began to light their myriad candles, the queenly full moon arose from her purple cushions.

Simon's Marketplace
Chester, Connecticut

Chester

Just returned from the Connecticut River—Chester, to be specific—and only minutes ahead of the showers and grumbly thunder and refracted sunbeams and towered, sooty cumulus. Hardly got wet enough to curl my whiskers or save me washing down *Moon Wind*. What good are all these summer showers when you still need to exert yourself to scrub the decks and the cockpit?

I took my son and his family aboard about noon on Wednesday—an early start—and we puttered out of Pine Island Sound into the force-three gale. We headed due west. The wind headed due east. The tide would be against us till nearly four. The choices were to motor to Old Saybrook, twelve miles upwind, or tack to Orient Point and back, adding at least two hours to our journey. As we meant to meet my other son at the mouth of the river, then ascend to East Haddam, hopefully during daylight, I opted for the motor.

The trip proved uneventful. My son and I played with my new GPS, and learned a couple of things. Such as, the course and distance to the next mark is taken from the position of the cursor. If the cursor is not replaced to the position you occupy, well . . . We learned that the QUIT button serves this important function and saves the tedium of scrolling and scrolling.

Not having a paper map of the river, I've always navigated this part of the world by memory, and kept to the ample channel going upstream. This is a conservative approach and, around the mouth of the river, necessary. There are quite a few gallons of shoal water all about Essex, Old Saybrook, and Old Lyme. Once you get to Deep River, there's so much water you can extravagate nearly from shore to shore. I, myself, have surprised any number of aircraft carriers snugly nestled beneath the silver maples . . .

We made the turn at bell number 8 off Long Sand Shoal beyond the mouth of the river and headed for the jetties. Now we should turn off the motor and sail close-reached. Except it was now past four o'clock—the hour when every breeze in Connecticut takes the evening off. I pushed the starter button again and we motored into the river. In company with three other sloops, we approached the railroad trestle. Six minutes until opening read the timer. Soon, the Amtrak Acela came roaring by, to the gratification of my grandson. The timer clicked down to zero and still we waited. After ten minutes I radioed the bridge tender: *MoonWind* to *Old Lyme Draw,* come in, please. Yes, he replied, they've messed my signals; there's another train on its way.

In ten minutes more, this train came through and soon the drawbridge opened. We motored to the public pier where my other son waited, tossed out our fenders, and made fast. By the time we cast off it was crowding six o'clock. We motored upriver feasting on smoked salmon and baguette. My grandson danced on the foredeck, and swashed any number of buckles.

The tide abetted us as we puttered nonchalantly past all the familiar places, lovelier now in the colorful, quiet light. I have never sated myself with my Connecticut. I hope to return with my kayak on board *MoonWind,* and make side trips into every cove and estuary one more time; pick some mallow flowers and pet some muskrats; listen to the blackbirds trill amid the cattails; see the large carp swirl in the backwaters; hear the song of the wind in the cottonwood trees.

We motored past Hadlyme Landing as dusk flung its muted canopy over the river. Our plan had been to ascend to Goodspeed's Landing in East Haddam, but my family had plans to meet with their mother for supper, and the evening came on quickly. Neither Gillette's landing nor the public wharves at Hadlyme exists anymore whatsoever. The Chester–Hadlyme Ferry chooses not to share her specialized slip—even with a local waterman.

But on the Chester bank above the ferry landing lies a tiny marina. Patronized by only powerboats, it boasts a snug but shallow basin and a very short fuel pier. We took some soundings as we crept up to this pier. As there proved sufficient water, we proceeded to tie up and unload our baggage. My sons instructed their mother where to meet them. We said our good-byes and I shoved off into the stream.

I prefer to anchor in daylight in case my hook doesn't hold. I puttered downriver a half mile and, just below the ferry landing, anchored by an undeveloped stretch of the Chester shore. The mist prevailed as night came on, and the nearly full moon shone gauzily, high above the muted, reflective river. The gray-green maples draped themselves with the dark. Not a voice, not a vehicle, presumed to disturb my idyll. Aside from a single night heron, I had the entire world to myself.

Black-crowned night heron

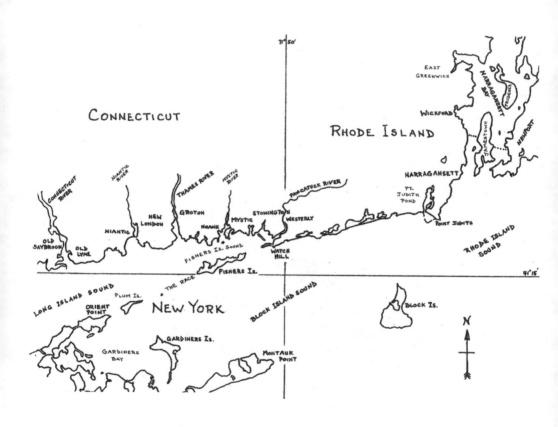

THE THAMES RIVER

Charter schooner "Mystic Whaler"

A Matter of Perspective

I've been sailing with my son and his family twice this week. Monday it blew a good fifteen knots and I refrained from hanking on my larger genoa. Even my 115 would prove more than enough, but within the shelter of the breakwater, it didn't seem all that fierce.

Once outside, the wind sufficed to heel us over twenty to thirty degrees, causing considerable consternation to four-year-old Jasper, whose water journeys have mostly been by canoe. He hung on tightly to anything within reach and inquired why we couldn't return to the dock.

Because we are having fun, we replied.

It's all a matter of perspective. I've been out when I needed to reef, but never been caught by a squall when I lost control. Perhaps, when that happens, some grown-up can reassure me.

A couple of hours sufficed on Monday to give us all an appetite for dinner. Safe in our slip, we stowed our gear, scrubbed the deck, and went off to the lobster pound. Jasper and his cousin, Kelly, were much consoled by the prospect of lobster dinner. The cats were consoled by leftover melted butter. And they hadn't even been asked along for the sail.

Thursday proved a glorious day: ten knots, calm seas, and sunshine by the bushel. The wind blew from the south. We had a close reach both coming and going along the Connecticut shore and made our way to the mouth of the Thames at New London. Jasper continued to request we return to the dock, but there was much less vehemence in his requests, and all of our passage he remained with me by the forward hatch as I pointed out the various boats and lighthouses.

"Look," I said. "There goes the high-speed ferry to Block Island."

A hydrofoil boat of fifty tons, she attains a speed of forty knots and throws a rooster tail ten feet tall.

And, marvel of marvels, out came a submarine from the navy base upriver, her long deck nearly awash. She headed south toward the Race at such a leisurely pace that we gained a mile for a better view before she slipped down and sought audience with the whales.

Then we saw the ferry to Orient Point depart the Thames as her sister ship hove into view, emerging from Gardiners Bay. The two of them met and curtsied and continued their opposite ways. That reminded us that my son and his family planned to take that ferry that afternoon, and we jibed *MoonWind* and reached our way toward Noank.

Now my focus must be to make *MoonWind* seaworthy before the first of the month. Paula flies to Rhodes in the Aegean then, and I shall sail eastward. I need to improve my facility with my handheld GPS and procure more charts. Once I secure my fuel tanks and their covers, I should refinish the brightwork on my Whitehall. I'll need her as my tender to go ashore as I can't afford a thousand dollars for docking fees over the two-week period.

The weather should be ideal the early portion of September. I anticipate a delightful trip, and homey harbors, and hospitable receptions. Already the wind has begun to be more constant. Hopefully, on my return, my notebook will bulge with tales of that mythical land to the east the natives named Massachusetts, meaning: "end of the world." Everyone from Connecticut knows that the sea stops just the other side of Newport, Rhode Island, and anyone who sails beyond inevitably falls off the edge of the earth. But when has skepticism deterred any constant waterman?

I hope to return and make charts proving that Woods Hole and Martha's Vineyard really exist. But aside from my being shanghaied by mermaids, you probably won't believe a thing I tell you.

The Gooseneck Clevis

Went out yesterday to play on the water and discovered a ten-knot breeze lurking off the harbor at New London. Problem was, it couldn't decide whether to blow on Connecticut or New York. Firstly, it backed about forty degrees, then veered ahead, then backed again, then nearly died altogether. I tried to ascend the Thames River, between New London and Groton. I scarcely made it as far as Ledge Light when the wind veered some more and blew straight down the river.

Well, I thought, perhaps I'll just head home. They've just reactivated the water on our piers and it wouldn't hurt to wash down *Moon-Wind* after a winter of indolence and grime. But the wind veered some more and I had to head out to sea a point or two more than I wanted. I decided to confer with Father Aeolus, lord of the winds. We agreed that if he let me sail to Noank parallel to the shore, I'd promise not to spill hot air as usual. Being glib, I fooled the poor old fellow once again. He backed the wind so far that I needed to jibe, and I ran before the breeze the whole way home.

When I reached West Cove, I jibed again and tucked in out of the weather. I put the helm down and dropped the mainsail into her lazy jacks. I can sail into my slip with just my genny, I reflected. Lord knows I need the practice. But I tilted the outboard into the drink and fired it up, just for assurance's sake. Nothing like a bit of assurance these days of rampant litigation. After the motor warmed up, I turned it off. I much prefer the sweet song of the herring gull to the growl of little pistons.

I was sprawled in the cockpit, wafting toward the channel, the genny drawing; making two knots and enjoying the mild weather, when I noticed the boom. Difficult not to notice something a yard above your head. But it had a twist to it that didn't seem quite right.

My boat has roller reefing: a worm gear assembly just abaft the gooseneck. You slip a handle onto the jackshaft, remove the track stop, slack the halyard, and crank the handle. The mainsail rolls up on the slowly revolving boom. Unhooking the boom vang often makes a difference. So does disconnecting the lazy jacks. Unless it's blowing thirty knots, it's seldom more trouble than folding your fractious elephant until he fits in your pocket.

Now the boom looked as though I hadn't left it true last time I furled the main. It was rotated several degrees. The advantage of a worm gear is that the driven pinion—the boom—can never rotate unless you activate the worm—i.e., crank the handle. But the boom had been true with the mainsail when I departed, and the handle was busily napping in its locker.

The explanation intruded itself on that dullness I call my mind. The clevis on the gooseneck had torn away from the slide during a flying gibe. Last week I had chosen to eat a granola bar and had tucked the tiller between my legs while surfing down four-footers before the wind. I had, of course, neglected to set my preventer. I barely avoided having the boom knock some common sense into my head.

The weld had all but parted. My boom was dangling by a tenth of its normal metal. I strove to imagine what might have happened had it parted in a serious wind with *MoonWind* surging though ragged seas, heeled over forty degrees. I often amuse myself in such a fashion.

I suddenly had no desire to tempt Poseidon further. I tiptoed forward, dropped the genny, and sedately motored the last quarter mile to my slip. There I removed the sail, the vang, the mainsheet, and the boom. As small things tend to amuse me, I made it a point to drop a little shackle over the side. I carried the boom to my truck and lashed it securely.

Then I spent time in rigging extra spring lines across the slip. A stern nor'easter with gusts to fifty knots is on the books for tomorrow. I keep a hundred-foot coil of three-quarters towline stowed in my locker. As no other boat was sharing my slip, I ran three lengths to the twelve-inch cleats on the opposite finger pier and tautened them until they kept *MoonWind* from striking the pier alongside. Then I doubled up all my usual lines, applied all the chafing gear I had on board, and adjusted my fenders. The fenders now seemed superfluous, but it seemed a bit foolish to leave them in the locker.

Peace of mind is what you earn for spending a few extra minutes securing your boat. If a hurricane comes, the piers may all go west. For a gentle breeze of fifty knots, some extra line suffices.

Thames Mouth

Yesterday we had a work party at our yacht club. I spent a good part of the morning scrubbing furniture, then washed down the patio deck with a long-handled brush. My niece followed me with the hose, pushing the dirt and soap ahead of me, and occasionally filling my sneaker with fresh water. At noon we gathered for lunch, indoors; the clubhouse now spotless, the meal delectable. The galley slaves cheerfully cleaned up afterward, then snuck off to work on their boats.

Moon Wind pranced in her temporary slip, and demanded petulantly that I take her out. The temperature had soared into the sixties. The breeze blew from the south-southeast at a moderate six knots. I bent on my larger genoa jib, a 150, and removed my boom cover. The outboard started immediately. I cast off and backed out of my slip and motored around the breakwater out to Avery Point.

The breeze was behind me as I hoisted both my sails, but it shifted over and back a couple of points all afternoon. I settled on a course before the wind, set my preventer, and began to study my chart.

My plan had been to ascend the Thames most of the way to Norwich, ten miles above the sound. But two small factors deterred me. The first was the wind—it died away to nearly the merest rumor. The second was the railroad trestle a couple of miles upriver. Thirty feet vertical clearance asserted my chart. *Moon Wind's* mast stands thirty-seven feet above the water. It would be a shame to snag my mast on the railroad bridge and knock it off its towers into the river. Had I been ambitious, I could have called the bridge tender and had him rear back his bascule on its pivot; but with such a light breeze, and such a late start, I would have been back to annoy him within the hour.

I resigned myself to playing about the ample mouth of the Thames.

Because of the navy base upriver and the shipyard at the mouth, the designated channel has forty feet of water—enough to sail *MoonWind* upside down. On a stormy day, that might have proved a consideration; today, I had to resign myself to sailing right-side up. But the Thames has adequate water, ten feet or more, nearly to each shore. This is a good thing to know when you need to tack.

Eventually, the wind picked up enough to swell my sails, and I wrinkled up the river at a rousing three knots. This allowed me the leisure to inspect the submarines being built on the east bank, and the lighthouse and old Fort Trumbull on the west. It also allowed me leisure to play tag with the various ferryboats that regularly ply the river.

Just behind the New London railroad station on the west bank, downstream from the State Pier, berth the large stately ferries to Orient Point. The high-speed trimaran ferry to Block Island also berths here, but doesn't run until summertime. A bit downstream lies the ferry to Fishers Island. I got to play hide and seek with most of these monsters. Fortunately, they're relegated to staying in the channel, so they hadn't much chance of catching little *MoonWind*.

Besides the ferries, there wasn't much traffic. A couple of powerboats went by and, above the bridge, I saw a few smaller sails. Electric Boat, which builds our submarines, has a small security vessel that patrols its waterfront. They carefully watched as I sailed by their massive piers where a submarine was tethered for repairs. I hoped I could sneak it into my cockpit locker when they weren't looking, and take it home for my grandson to play with next time he comes to visit, but their vigilance deterred me.

I came about at the railroad trestle and tacked back down the river. The breeze sufficed to heel me over twenty degrees and I had a delightful sail. I descended to the now unmanned old brick lighthouse at New London Ledge. This historic landmark is a cubical brick edifice of Second Empire design. The last light keeper hanged himself from a rafter and the lighthouse is properly haunted.

With numerous short tacks, I avoided the shoals and entered Pine Island Sound. Behind Pine Island, I rounded up and dropped my mainsail into her lazy jacks. I kicked my fenders over the side and wafted back to my slip with only my genny. The one other boat at the yacht club piers is four slips up from me. Her sail cover was buttoned down; her fetters were all made fast. The reproachful look she bestowed on us over her shoulder as we rippled by her was sad to see. I had to reprimand *Moon Wind* severely for chortling.

PINE ISLAND SOUND

Avery Point Light, Groton, Connecticut

Independence Day

Every Independence Day—give or take a couple of weeks—the Mashantucket Pequot tribe hosts a fireworks display. As these people own a flourishing casino here in Connecticut, they can afford the best. The fireworks are launched from three barges anchored off old Fort Trumbull, now a state park, a couple of miles above the mouth of the Thames River.

Although the show commences at half past nine, by midafternoon boats are flocking to the site and jostling for advantage. When the fireworks end, every vessel storms downriver to avoid being caught in the crush. Skippers ignore their wakes. Within a few minutes, the turbulence at the river mouth resembles the worst sort of tidal rip imaginable. It's no place to be in a twenty-six-foot sailboat plodding along at four knots in the dark.

Our game plan has been to join our friends on their Egg Harbor 33, which they anchor near the mouth of the river, a mile or so away from the display. The view is superb, the reports of the grand finale don't stunt your hearing, and you're out of the river before the madness begins.

Our friends keep their boat at Shennecossett Yacht Club, just around Avery Point at the mouth of the Thames and tucked behind the shelter of Pine Island. As it's only four miles from Noank where we moor *MoonWind,* we took a leisurely Saturday morning and got under way after lunch. There wasn't much wind and we had to buck the tide, so it took us two hours to reach Pine Island Sound. Sailing is not a sport for the impatient.

We'd been assigned a transient slip with finger piers rather than one with pilings. Not only did this facilitate mooring, but meant we hadn't needed to bring our giraffe to stand on the walkway and hoist our huge cooler up and over the bow pulpit. Our giraffe has issues with *MoonWind*'s headroom.

We lugged our cooler up to the picnic grounds beside the club-house and did our best to lighten it. After eating several smidgeons too much we recuperated aboard the Egg Harbor before shoving off for the Thames. At half past eight, we departed for the two-mile trip beyond the unexplored waters by Avery Point. We anchored in eight-een feet off Eastern Point. As the tide and wind both ascended the river, our cockpit faced upstream for a perfect view. We opened some folding chairs and put our feet up. Then we let our hair down. As I haven't much left, this didn't take me long.

Fortunately, our revelations were interrupted by the most magnif-icent fireworks show I ever remember seeing. It's wonderful what bar-rels of money can do, but in forty minutes the money barrels were empty. The shock from the finale must have been felt as far away as Chicago. We were glad to be anchored a mile from the concussion. We hoisted our hook while under way and roared off into the dark. We ac-celerated to twenty knots. Even so, boats from up the river hurtled by us. In just a few minutes, we throttled down and tucked behind Pine Island.

Sunday morning the two of us emptied *MoonWind* and scrubbed her soundly, inside and out. Keeping her on a mooring has its draw-backs, one of which is access to fresh water. After two hours, we'd had enough fun and were wet to the waist as well. Playing the hose on each other helped. We filled the water tank and stowed our gear. As we departed, we stopped at the fuel pier to pump out our holding tank. The club attendant asked if we wanted to flush our tank with fresh water and pump it again. Yes, indeed! The courtesy at Shen-necossett leaves nothing to be desired.

We motored out past Pine Island and quickly raised our main and a midsize genny. There was just enough breeze to keep them swelled, but the tide ebbed in our favor. We made three knots; the sea rippled gently by us. Halfway home, off Seaflower Reef, we encountered a bit more breeze. We accelerated to four knots, then to five. We even heeled over. We made six knots. By the time we came to Noank, we tore along at seven knots over the ground.

"Let's sail to Latimer Reef and back," said Paula.

Halfway there we hit eight knots; the sea rose up; the tide shoved hard. The wind blew a steady twenty. We topped out at 8.3 knots over the ground. We never did less than seven. Not bad for a boat with a hull speed of just six knots. Our hair grew stiff with spray. As I hadn't bothered to take a reef, I was forced to dump wind; else I would slew upwind and lose control.

Coming back against the tide we managed a bit over four knots; the effects were much the same. When *MoonWind* leans more than forty degrees with that much canvas on her, the rudder won't hold her on course. I could have reefed or taken in my small genoa, but going to Latimer Reef and back was only an extra five miles. Besides—I needed to rinse my outhaul in salt water.

Cloudy with a Chance of Muskrats

A damp, dreary, chilly, lamentable day. Cloudy with a chance of muskrats, as my grandmother used to say. But today I moved *Moon-Wind* from the marina to the yacht club via Fishers Island Sound, which is not known for abundant reserves of muskrats.

At five o'clock, in steady rain, I was at the helm in my foul-weather gear, backing out of my slip at Spicer's Marina. Messing about and getting my sails soaked for an hour's passage made no sense. The tide assisted me; the wind was abeam at six to eight knots; my motor recited her lines without a stutter. Visibility was limited: at three miles, the ferry to Orient Point appeared a muted, gray-green specter, silently fading into the distant mist. At ten to six, I nosed *MoonWind* into her slip in the shelter of Pine Island, took her forward mooring line, stepped down onto the finger pier, and snubbed her before she could nuzzle up to the walkway.

They've assigned me this temporary slip at Shennecossett Yacht Club while I wait to be assigned a permanent mooring. First they need to notify all the owners of present moorings, to determine how many members intend to use them. Last season several remained untenanted. As there is no extra space to put down any new moorings, I shall have to purchase the ground tackle from a member who no longer plans to moor his or her vessel, else purchase my own to replace it. A new, three-hundred-pound mushroom anchor, plus chain and pendants and shackles and mooring buoy, will cost me a thousand dollars. I'll pay four hundred dollars to have it installed.

Then I have to purchase a set of jack stands. Even secondhand, they'll cost me a few hundred dollars. This summer I'll haul *Moon-Wind,* for the first time in three years, and see how her bottom fares. In order to keep her in the drink another thirty-six months, I'll need to spend a couple of hundred dollars on bottom paint.

I'll have to sell a lot of books this summer . . .

I'll also need to pull *MoonWind's* stick to replace the masthead light and insulate inside the mast so the wiring doesn't continuously rap, and replace my halyards and at least inspect my standing rigging and possibly replace it. That would be another thousand dollars just for materials. At least I can do all the work myself. Otherwise, I'd never be able to afford to keep any boat much larger than my Whitehall.

Speaking of whom, she presently resides inside my garage. At least I repaired and varnished her last spring, and she hasn't been exposed to sun or weather. But I need to build a new axle to move her about and to load her into my truck. Now that I think about it, she needs at least one coat of bottom paint. My kayak, bless her, doesn't require a thing except a good scrubbing.

What with writing, illustrating, promoting, and selling books, taking care of my boats and this house and the yard, I wonder that I have any time to work. Work at a *paying* job, that is. Because everyone wants my money. It's very generous of them, of course, to relieve me of the burden of having to spend it on myself, but sometimes, only sometimes, I wish I had enough to go around. I send the telephone company two or three dollars and they respond with an angry letter. I give the doctor a ten-dollar bill, or at least a five and four singles, and he wants to know about the odd hundred dollars. It's very provoking of him, to say the least, when he ought to know that *MoonWind* needs a new anchor.

If all these people would only leave me alone, I shouldn't have to work so much in the boatyard, applying varnish to grab rails with my beard and rebedding old mizzen halyards. Then I'd maybe have enough time to work on my memoirs. This is serious business. I meet at least two people each month who compliment me on my last journal entry. If that isn't encouragement, nothing is.

My goal this year is to sell the remainder of the two thousand books my publisher had printed. Then I can deliver my next book of journals to him. It's a self-perpetuating business—rather like life. You have to write books to publish books to sell books to write books. With any luck, a reader or two gets tangled up in the process. Hopefully, the occasional small royalty gets hung up in my pocket.

I love the folks who come up to me after a reading and tell me how much they enjoy my stories, then walk out the door, get in their cars, and go home without my book. I can only hope that their televisions suffer astigmatism, and that termites conspire to eat their library cards.

Shennecossett Yacht Club

Drive-in Movies

We go to the Christmas eggnog party at Shennecossett Yacht Club. Roast beef and ham and shrimp and conviviality and eggnog with rum and conviviality and, after attempting conviviality with boat folk for a while, I slip away into the dark to commiserate with *MoonWind*.

She's on the hard for the first time in years and she isn't happy about it. The past three winters she spent in the drink, communing with the cormorant and waiting those lapses 'twixt ice and snow when I'd most be apt to take her out for an afternoon to visit with the seals.

And now she's propped on seven jack stands a hundred yards from the sea and, much as she wriggles, she can't get down to flop her way back to the water.

"Why are you doing this to me?" she says.

"Well," I say, "your bottom sadly needs scrubbing, lass. And I need to repair that gouge in your keel where you tried to seduce that rock. And you could use a new depth sounder. And then we have to give you a few more coats of bottom paint so you won't have to leave the water for three more years."

She listens to me patiently and gives a little shrug.

"If I must, I must," she says. She settles onto her poppets with a sigh.

I fondle her bottom lovingly and return to the noisy room. A hundred people are talking all at once. It isn't nearly so restful as an evening on the ocean. I slop a little more eggnog into my cup and wander about, looking for someone innocent on whom to inflict myself.

The river rat with the grizzled whiskers nods to me and I heave to for a spell. As a lad he was out on the water every chance, racing small powerboats, sailing around Long Island Sound, and terrorizing what used to be staid little towns along the shore. He now has a good-size sloop and a lovely first mate and time enough to enjoy them both together. Not only that, but he seems to enjoy my blather. It's his only shortcoming I know of so I tend to overlook it.

We speak of boats and the river and the villages whose innocence is imperiled by rampant tourism. We speak of picking up moorings in foreign ports where the natives speak their own unintelligible language—Massachusetts, for instance.

We speak of our lengthy boyhoods, which are coming to their close. Peter Pan with white whiskers seems to lack in credibility. Once, long ago, we could fly to mysterious worlds or romp throughout the various towns about the mouth of the river with impunity. We speak of the local places we used to frequent. He mentions the movie theater in his town—now bulged by a boutique. There used to be a movie house in most of these little towns.

"Remember the drive-in movie over in Clinton?" he says.

"Yes," I say. "And the one in Middletown and the one in Portland."

"I used to go to the drive-ins on my motorcycle," he says.

I wink at him. "*I* used to go to the drive-ins in my boat."

His wife looks at me, wide-eyed.

"You used to go to the drive-ins in your boat?"

"Well," I say. "You had to be cautious and keep your weather eye upon your depth sounder. I'd pick a spot in the last row so I didn't have to tack among the parked cars. Then I'd make fast to one of the stanchions that had the speakers on it. If it was windy I'd stream an anchor astern so I wouldn't swing."

Her eyes grow larger and larger.

"Is he serious?" she asks her amiable husband.

"I should think so," he says. "Matthew and I grew up on the river messing about in boats. There aren't many places a serious messer can't take his boat if he tries."

"*I* think you're being facetious," she says to me.

I smile at her. "I would never tell you anything that wasn't entirely true," I say. "After all, I'm a sailor, and everyone knows that sailors never lie."

"Well," she says. "I can see how it might be possible."

"I won't deceive you," I say to her, "it wasn't a very large boat. You wouldn't want to try it with that forty-foot sloop of yours. My boat drew only four feet. "

"You guys," she says. "It always amazed me how roisterous those drive-in theaters got—positively turbulent."

"It was all of us boaters," I say to her, "lined up at the popcorn booth in our dinghies and backing water."

"Yes," she says. "That must have been the cause of it."

"You shouldn't roll your eyes so far," I say to her. "What if they stuck like that?"

Taking the Plunge

Well, *MoonWind* finally took the plunge this Thursday. After five months on the hard after three years at large she was getting restless. It grieved me to see her squirm to get free of her poppets to no avail.

"Why am I up here? What have I done that was so bad?" she asked.

"After three years in the drink," I told her, "I need to check your bottom."

"Hmmphh!" she said. "I bet you tell all the girls that."

Nevertheless, I began by mending her keel (I told you not to play on that rock pile, lass). A bit of glass cloth, a bit of matting, a bit of resin, a bit of epoxy undercoat, several fifty-grit sanding pads, a couple of swipes of bottom paint, and all was pretty once more. Only two coats of ablative bottom paint had worn away of the four she had started with three years ago. Except for a couple of minor abrasions, the indicator coat and the next above it were basically intact. Two more coats ensure she won't need to visit the hard for at least three, maybe even four more years.

Life on the hard leaves much to be desired. Those fair winter days that punctuate the solemnity ever entice *MoonWind's* venturesome nature. Off we go to visit the seals or follow the slant of light to its pale lair.

But I'm wandering from the point of the present story.

As soon as I'd finished ministering to *MoonWind's* curvaceous bottom I climbed aboard and tended to her brightwork.

Much as I admire brightwork on boats, no one knows better the endless travail to make it appear pristine. After eight coats of spar varnish, my grab rails and hatch surrounds reflected the April sun. My drop boards glowed after dark.

Then I did what I'd threatened these past five years and purchased two decals proclaiming MOONWIND and glued them to her quarters. Their copper color contrasts nicely with her hunter-green hull. *Moon-Wind* was so proud of herself and strained so hard to look over her shoulder to admire her new decals that she nearly fell off her poppets. Ah, the vanity of little sailboats! Now hold still, my girl, while I wax your hull.

I then reeved new halyards, replaced my anchor light, and polished my mast. I opened the hood of my pickup truck, connected my jumper cables to the battery, and tested all the light fixtures on my mast. I spoke sweetly to my outboard motor and stroked her till she purred. I changed both fuel filters, cleaned the oil filter, changed the oil and lower end grease, and sanded the anode clean.

I rigged some dock lines, slung my new fenders over the side, and smiled at the yard crew. These amiable fellows lifted *Moon Wind* gently off her jack stands and lowered her ever so easily into the harbor. I have to admit I actually watched her wiggle her toes in the water.

Then we stepped her mast. Beside the lazy jacks finding themselves on the wrong side of the starboard shrouds, everything went well. I even remembered to shut all my through-hull fittings and connect my hoses.

My outboard started as soon as I admired its starting button. I backed out of the lift slip and motored slowly 'round the end of B pier and down to slip 46. Here I secured for the weekend while I finished rigging and wiring. Monday I go on my mooring. Meanwhile, I need to empty *Moon Wind* and scrub her every inch. I need to restring the VHF cable from the mast to my radio, aft. I need to connect all my mast lights, scrub my water tank, and top off the electrolyte in my battery. A real sailor's work is seldom done. Cleaning the bilge with your toothbrush merely prepares for stowing the tons of gear you need to convince your boat that you take her seriously.

For, after all, the point to all this nonsense is to sail off into the sunset so, whatever you do, don't forget your sunglasses.

Three Mile Harbor

This weekend Shennecossett Yacht Club invited its members to participate in a weekend rendezvous at Three Mile Harbor in East Hampton, New York. Though not normally fans of group carousals, we ventured forth to join in, mostly in the hope of exploring a harbor new to us. The eighteen miles were pretty much into the wind that wasn't blowing, so we opted to motor without even raising our sails.

Of course, we had to pass through the Race—that five miles of broken water between Orient Point and Fishers Island. We chose to go by the Sluiceway, between Plum Island and Great Gull Island—both within the Race. Being the most direct route to our destination, it obviously had sufficient current to make for a bouncy passage. Fortunately, the rip was only three knots against us, and we powered through without mishap. The three-foot chop sufficed to keep us awake. On a rough day, during the brunt of the tide, this passage can be a nuisance.

Once we were through, we sailed down the backside of Gardiners Island toward Three Mile Harbor, about six miles across Gardiners Bay. Lobster pot buoys abounded in our path, meaning I couldn't doze off at the helm. The First Mate lay fast asleep on the starboard locker.

By seventeen hundred, we fetched the mid-channel marker for our harbor—a tall red-and-white bell. Three large black-backed gulls stood sentry on it, mere inches from the gently striking clapper—music to their avian brains no doubt.

We motored down the long channel, heeding advice not to turn into the anchorage till way past the sandy spit by the harbor mouth. Although this morsel of land has a house upon it, its sandbar extends a half mile to the south. The channel follows the left—that is, the east—bank, upon which are two sizable marinas. Dozens and dozens of proud vessels have their moorings in this harbor, and many more come to anchor as we would.

We found our comrades—maybe a dozen boats—already moored, some rafted together in clumps of three. We were urged to find a transient mooring—with or without a companion to share the cost. Not being acquainted with many members, we chose to swing by ourselves on our anchor and save the seventy-five dollars. This is the highest rate that I've met to rent a transient mooring. Imagine: paying three times the total price of Manhattan to spend one night in a harbor.

A cocktail party was scheduled aboard three forty-foot sloops rafted together nearby. This proved the opportunity to try our new gate and boarding ladder for getting aboard the Whitehall. Rather than crawl beneath the lifeline and roll into our dinghy, we now could descend in a grand and deliberate style down three steps. The trick was to have sufficient fenders to keep the Whitehall's bright teak rail from eating *MoonWind*'s hull.

We rowed our shrimp and cocktail sauce and bottle of wine the hundred yards to the party, and left the Whitehall to brag amid the crowd of inflatable dinghies.

The party was a success, as parties go. Forty people clambered from boat to boat to boat and talked the varnish off what little brightwork these new yachts sported. There was food and more food and drink and enough to spare. Or there should have been. After an hour we came away satiated. An hour of people stepping on my ears now satisfies my quota for conviviality. The older I grow, the more I cherish my time alone—especially on the water. An occasional function at the clubhouse where I have good conversation with three or four people suffices to keep me from becoming a total curmudgeon. I always thought I'd prefer to go to heaven after I die, only because of the scarcity of its inhabitants.

Now it's mid-Saturday-morning. Leaving my First Mate to guard the drop boards, I take the Whitehall to forage after more ice. I wend among the moored boats, admiring rigs and the woodwork on older vessels. I poke into a small basin containing some fifty small yachts and find nobody to converse with save a pair of talkative terns on a bearded piling. There seem to be no facilities ashore. I pull back to the harbor and follow the shoreline north. At East Hampton Point Marina, I draw the Whitehall alongside a float and tie off between two pilings. If you want cleats in Three Mile Harbor you have to bring them with you. After I see the posted price for transient slips, it occurs to me that perhaps the cleats are solid gold and are kept locked up until asked for.

The ship's store has coffee and pastry, fancy T-shirts and ball caps, and lots of floating toys. There seems to be little in the way of line and hardware, paint and varnish, and useful sailorly stuff. Perhaps the folks over here don't use such trifles. The bags of ice were little more extortionate than elsewhere so I bought twenty pounds and tucked it into the Whitehall. The posted, daily use of a slip is $6.50 per foot— the price of a decent hotel room—but you need to supply your own hotel and the room service as well. I've been told that you can get a decent lunch at the marina restaurant for merely one hundred dollars a couple—not including the tip.

I made my escape before they could charge me dockage for my Whitehall, and pulled back to *MoonWind* to feast on lemonade and egg salad sandwiches. I guess I'm not cut out for the yachty life. On my way back I circled a lithe and lovely old yawl built all of wood and resplendent with gallons of varnish. About thirty feet long and double-ended, she harked to a day of lavishness and splendor. A lovely lady but not one I'd care to keep up.

By late afternoon, the SYC contingent had loaded their dinghies with grills and charcoal and steaks and beer and puttered the mile to Sammy's Beach for a picnic. We followed them sedately in the Whitehall. I won't profane my pulling boat with a motor. Rowing her is more fun than most of the picnics I've attended. One of the dinghies offered me a tow, and I smiled graciously as I refused. If I don't wear some varnish off my slim spruce oars, what'll I do off-season for entertainment?

Once at the beach, the members began a series of parlor games. Even with lubrication I had no interest in joining in. This seems to be de rigueur for yacht club rendezvous: silly games and silly hats and silly awards and sacrificial cows consigned to the flames.

Meanwhile, the tide came in and then came in and then came in some more until our piece of beach was awash and coolers went adrift and sea serpents came and went among the moored dinghies. We loaded our gear and wended our placid way against the breeze until we nestled against the flank of our dozing *Moon Wind*. After a rigorous afternoon of watching others disport themselves, we needed a bit of a nap. When we awoke it was nearly half past breakfast.

In the afternoon, a breeze sprang accoutered as Athena from Zeus and bore us swiftly home. The allure of a weekend with many congenial people is now so appalling, I doubt I will ever go sailing again with anyone save my cat.

Thanksgiving Day 2009

Seems the season—the boating season, that is—is winding down. Went to a shindig at the boat club Sunday and everyone was talking about how their boats are up on the hard and what, maybe, they might just do next summer. Me, I've got my boats—both of 'em—in the water still. I'll sail *Moon Wind* over to Noank this Wednesday to winter wet, and row the Whitehall over the next fair day. Supposed to be blowing thirty knots next weekend—not great rowing weather.

People ask, don't you ever get ice in your slip at Noank? Doesn't your sloop get iced in? Most I've seen is a couple of inches, three or four winters back. All I did was bust it up with a vagrant two-by-four. Seems in the past they used to have real winter. Folks at the yacht club were talking Sunday about their fathers walking across the sound to Fishers Island, two miles and more offshore. I've heard tell of people driving their cars across. Musta been back at the end of the previous ice age—maybe twelve thousand years ago—give or take a woolly mammoth or two.

Anyway, the temperature here in Connecticut is more redolent of April than of November—high fifties during the day, just above freezing at night. Another week and it ought to be sugaring weather . . .

Took *Moon Wind* home to Noank yesterday. Motor started with no complaints and enjoyed the fresh tank of fuel. I bent on my smaller genoa and left the mainsail covered. There seemed to be almost no breeze. The harbor was so placid that when I removed all my mooring lines, *Moon Wind* just sat like a sleepy duck with her head beneath her wing.

"Time to get up and fly, lass," I said, and gentled her out of her slip. I motored round Pine Island and I clambered forward and hoisted the genoa jib. There was barely breeze enough to keep it filled. I turned off the motor and watched the tide negate any progress we made. And the breeze blew out of the east—the way I needed to go. After fifteen minutes of flopping about, I dropped the jib and turned the motor back on. Some days it hardly pays to hoist your sails. I motored out to the west side of North Dumpling and looked about.

A bit of haze limited my visibility to maybe six miles but, even so, I could plainly discern eight lighthouses of the ten visible from this point. To see the Stonington, Connecticut lighthouse, now a museum, you need a clear day and maybe binoculars. The alternating red and white flashing lights from Watch Hill Light can be seen even on an overcast day when the building itself appears indistinct. Latimer Reef, between Stonington and Fishers Island, can be seen for miles. I could also see, with my naked eye, Morgan Point Light at Noank, North Dumpling, close aboard, and Race Rock Light. Little Gull Light, maybe six miles west, just east of Plum Island, I had to strain to locate. Ledge Light at the mouth of the Thames, New London Harbor Light on the New London shore, and Avery Point Light on the opposite bank stood two to three miles off. On a clear day all ten of these are readily discernible. Perhaps a mile or two to the west I might also descry Montauk Point Light, Orient Point Light, and Plum Island Light. I'll let you know.

Thanksgiving morning I took advantage of the tide and another windless day to move my Whitehall. A five-mile row before you gorge on too much Thanksgiving dinner can be a good thing—it whets the edge of gluttony and fosters true thankfulness. Or perhaps we should all go rowing after our feast. Burn off a few hundred calories so we needn't let out our trousers.

Fishers Island Sound proved merely a millpond—water so still I could see my reflection—always cause for alarm. The still, still surface was punctuated by fowl: loons, and mergansers, and cormorants by the dozens, and other birds I couldn't identify, not having had the foresight to remember my field glasses.

I rounded Bluff Point, crossed Mumford Cove, rounded Groton Long Point, and traversed the depth of West Cove to the marina. This winter I have the luxury of a double slip all to myself. *Moon Wind* and the Whitehall share a dance hall between two finger piers. Other years I've tucked the Whitehall underneath *Moon Wind*'s bow, but I needed to take great pains when docking not to trample my dinghy. Unless I rig a cover on the Whitehall, I'll have to haul her before she fills with sleet and snow and ice. At least she's easy to launch again if I feel the need of a row come February. Messers About never quite know just when such an urge may overtake them.

First Spring Sail

"So," I said to the old fellow on the pier, "do you like her?"

He was studiously admiring my friend's twenty-nine-foot sloop.

"She's lovely," he said. "Her brightwork is gorgeous."

"Would you like to buy her?" I asked.

"Is she yours?" he inquired.

"No," I said, "but let's not quibble about unimportant details. I'll give you a very good price. Her owners don't take her out more than a hundred days per season—they'll never miss her."

"That's all right," he said. "I already own a Bristol 29.9 and I'm in love with her. I'm just walking the piers, admiring boats. There's a pretty little sloop down by the end with a beautiful new deckhouse. I thought she might be a Grampion, but the port lights seem too small. Lovely old boat."

"Hunter-green hull?" I asked him. "Bristol-beige deckhouse?"

"That's right," he said.

"Come on," I said. "I'll take you aboard for a bit—I'm about to go out."

"You're going sailing?" he said. "On April first?"

"Sure," I said. "It's fifty degrees and blowing eight knots. What more could a sailor ask?"

We climbed aboard *Moon Wind,* went below, and talked about boats for a while. Then I pitched him overboard, bent on my smaller genoa, started my motor, and began to gather my dock lines. I left the two to windward, buckled my safety harness over my wet suit, put on my life jacket, woolly cap, and sunglasses, and gave a sailorly squint at the wind vane aloft. I stood on the finger pier, uncleated my last two dock lines and tossed them aboard, walked *Moon Wind* half out of her slip, seized the lower shroud, and hopped aboard. I put the motor into reverse, cleared the slip, shifted gear, and puttered into the channel, air horn at hand.

Within the breakwater all lay serene. I met a Fishers Island skiff entering the harbor and exchanged a wave with the woman at the wheel. Hers was the only vessel I was to see all afternoon, save for the ferries that repeatedly ply from New London to Fishers Island and Orient Point.

Soon as I cleared Mouse Island I hoisted my jib and killed the motor. Ah, Quietude! Ah, Bliss! Why even raise the main? I had three hours of good daylight to wend five miles downwind—down to Pine Island Sound, my destination. I wouldn't be returning—not today. So what if the tide ran against me? I wafted along at two knots and admired the herring gulls.

You may consider gulls raucous, and they are. You may consider gulls gluttonous, and they are. You may even think that their manners are less than genteel, and you'll be right. Now consider your normal, less-than-average *Homo sapiens,* who scarce deserves the second half of his name; who pollutes and litters, and argues his life away. And when was the last time you watched him skim the ocean on graceful wings just for the joy of it?

You need take things as you find them in this world. Excepting yourself, whom you're more than free to nurture, amaze, and alter. For life unwinds at a rapid rate, and the bitter end of your line won't be secured. So enjoy the gull as she rides the wind and smile when she leaves a few crab legs on your deck.

Blithely, as the afternoon cooled and the modest sun reclined, I reached around the far side of Pine Island and tucked behind the breakwater. I slacked my jib and the current whisked me between the pier and the seawall of the university. I put the helm down, and *Moon-Wind,* eager to be back at home, bounded into her slip with enthusiasm. I leapt down to the finger pier, almost in time to snub her dock line before she climbed the walkway. Now poor *MoonWind* needs a fresh chip of hunter-green paint on her proud, impetuous bow. Ah, little boats! When will they ever learn?

DIVAGATIONS, ABERRATIONS, AND DOWNRIGHT LIES

SNAGGED!

Snagged!

Every boat is entitled to snag one lobster pot warp in her travels. *MoonWind's* rudder mounts on her skeg with scarcely clearance between. Somehow, a bight of a pot warp managed to insinuate itself between the two above the lower bearing where the clearance is more ample.

Suddenly my forward progress ceased. Fortunately, the breeze was weak and my sails merely slatted about. I fished out the straining warp with my boat hook and attempted to free it from the rudder. Then I tipped my outboard into the drink and attempted to back up—perhaps pull from a different direction. Steering proved difficult.

This is when you should toss your mermaid over the side and make her earn her keep. My mermaid went on sabbatical and left me to my devices. These proved a bit less than adequate. The pot buoy bobbed behind me; a long length of three-eighths Manila tethered me to it. I wondered whether a lobster pot was jammed against my bottom. Something was. Eventually I asked pardon of the lobsterman and severed his warp.

The helm seemed a bit stiff, and the lobsters affected my steering. I vowed I would take my revenge with melted butter. Fortunately, I had but five miles to traverse. By bending my tiller I managed to make the full turn to get into my slip and made her fast. From the finger pier, I could discern another small buoy tucked against my rudder. No wonder she favored a starboard helm. But the lobsters had refrained from hitching a ride.

I tried to remove this buoy with my boat hook. That provided me entertainment for fifteen or twenty minutes. Tomorrow, I vowed, I'm diving down there, my knife between my teeth in true mariner fashion, and deal with the problem. Hopefully, to deal with the solution as well.

The following day, I drowned myself several times without much success. I did manage to come away with a pretty white Styrofoam buoy with a blue stripe around it. Now I have something to hang on my garage like all the other guys. However, a piece of cordage remained jammed between my rudder and skeg. The skipper of the old red ketch at the end of the pier came by to cheer me on. He happens to be a professional diver. He kicked off his sandals, took off his T-shirt, and hopped in.

"Give me your knife for a minute," he said.

On his third attempt, he surfaced with a bit of cord in his hand. Easy as that.

"Of course, my minimum fee for diving is $150," he cheerily informed me.

I unshipped my tiller and stove in my piggy bank. Wouldn't be the last time.

Last weekend he came groveling for a favor.

"I need you to fix my anchor light," he explained.

I strapped myself into the bosun's chair as he took a third turn on the winch with his main halyard.

"Just be sure to have fun up there," he reminded me.

I'd like to catch the fellow who designed that anchor light. The dome was through-bolted; the nuts so recessed that neither a wrench nor nut driver proved possible. A little pair of needle-nose vise grips finally did the job. I dropped the three number six nuts four times, but caught each on the second bounce. I had fun enough to share with several people. Turns out, a faulty connection had caused the problem. Took me mere minutes to fix it. Replacing the dome took only another half hour.

Her skipper was truly appreciative, but you should have seen his eyes roll when I handed him my bill.

The Journals of Constant Waterman

It's three degrees this morning; nearly cold enough to slake my craving to venture upon the water. My lovely sloop, *MoonWind,* huddles in her slip with nary a blanket.

The Pusslet sits on my desk, dipping her paw in what's left of my French roast, then blissfully licking her toes. A little caffeine goes a long way with the Pusslet. Having taken communion she walks between my monitor and keyboard, pausing to urge on the cursor with her nose.

I pat her corner of the desk beside the printer. Come and lie down, I say, and be a good girl. I worry she'll inadvertently tread on my keyboard. She carefully avoids it, but things are just a bit crowded. Her editing skills are various: She stands on the DELETE key or chews on my red pencil. Now she comes and lies down. I stroke her head, wipe her nose smears from the screen, and begin a new paragraph.

The fires are roaring below, the furnace adding its voice to the milieu. All our resource and defiance of the cold labor at keeping the monsters of winter at bay. I've been outside to feed the birds and bring in chunks of oak to feed to the fire. Though brisk, the air was still, and it wasn't cold enough to hurt to breathe. Rather a lovely morning—like biting into a tart and crunchy apple—maybe a Red Delicious.

The woodpile diminishes. There seems to be some correlation between the cold and it; some understanding I'm not quite privy to. I saw and split and stack the wood; the house grows cold; the woodpile shrinks; the house becomes a bit warmer. After all these years, this fire should have grown up and gotten a job. Instead, it remains on my hearth and squalls for breakfast. What would you like this morning, dear? Why don't you try an armload of yummy beechwood?

Today I signed a contract with my publisher and posted it, certified mail. Now I need to concentrate on completing illustrations for my book. Made one of the Loch Ness monster that looks exactly like her. Also one of our old, now demolished boat shop—a shot from the entry looking up at the peak—with the stern of a Stonington Pulling Boat jutting above the doorway. Another of the Hadlyme–Chester Ferry approaching her slip.

Found an advertisement last night for land on Cape Breton Island: forty acres for sixteen thousand dollars. It might be a viable option for retirement; the winters are not much frostier than here. The Gulf Stream shares its mildness with the shores of the North Atlantic. Inserted Halifax in my weather site and looked at mean temperatures throughout the year. About eight degrees cooler the whole year round, with lots of precipitation winter-long. A winter conducive to writing lengthy books. Or sailing south.

But the boating there should be glorious during the summer. Sounds and harbors abound. I imagine there are plenty of snug holes to shelter in, though the coast is probably rocky. The elevation on Cape Breton Island rises to over a quarter mile in places. Not exactly a sand dune.

I'd probably want to follow the seals south come Christmastime. Cape Breton Island lies five degrees of latitude, or three hundred nautical miles, north of the Connecticut shore, but a good deal farther, following the coast. It would certainly be a pleasant jaunt, and I'd get to inflict myself on the state of Maine. When I arrived in Connecticut I would need to live aboard if I sell this house.

I have no doubt I can continue writing memoirs of ships and harbors and seals and serpents until I grow too old to sail my boat. Then I shall write only sea stories made up out of whatever's left of my mind.

I see myself, in decrepitude, living aboard, tied up in some marina; venturing out with younger folk who are willing to put up with a crusty codger. At night I shall sit in my cockpit and gaze at the sea— that wondrous, live, and fathomless breadth of beauty—until the moon sets, when my faithful mermaid lays aloft and helps me below to my bunk.

A Reluctant Spring

It seems a reluctant spring. Even though the crocuses have been up for weeks; even though the daffodils have begun to open, the temperature still falls well into the twenties each night, and the Pusslets ask to come back in at half past six for breakfast with cold ears and their tails fully fluffed. It generally soars into the forties before midmorning. The sun comes out and it promises to be glorious. By the time I get to the boatyard, it has clouded over, the wind is blowing, and I'm hunkered within my hooded sweatshirt, wondering if this weekend bodes well for sailing.

I've been out four times this winter. Now that it's spring, I shouldn't be making a fuss. The mermaids—I mean the seals—have done basking on the rocks and have returned to the Maritime Provinces where it isn't so oppressively hot in April. Of course, they all have extremely warm and fashionable sealskin coats, for which they each paid some exorbitant price—as you, too, paid for your extremely thin skin.

I've been thinking how cold-intolerant I've become with approaching age. Maybe that's why I'm considering moving to the Maritime Provinces. I've never been gifted with the art of clever decisions. It's taken me all this while to decide that I should write, and look at the results.

I've written so much that I haven't had the time for more than two marriages. Written so much that I needed to paint four coats of ablative bottom paint on *MoonWind* to avoid having to take the time to haul her every winter. Written so much that I'm forced to arise at the crack of dawn to indulge my filthy habit. It's gotten so that my friends have begun to talk—something that could have been avoided had I had the sense not to tell them where I'd published my articles.

This is supposed to be a forum where I muse—or rant—about

boats. Sometimes I find myself writing of other things. This is a sign that I need to get out on the water again and drown my youthful inhibitions and tendencies to reflect. There are plenty of sunlit pools to perform that function. But I've nearly given up walking in the woods. There was a time when I could be happy sitting by a tiny stream in a shady grove.

Now I want to count the whitecaps ruffling the harbor. And sail off to foreign shores—maybe even as far as Massachusetts. Even though the folks there are just a bit strange and use an alphabet with fewer consonants, good times can be had. Most everyone is friendly, and would just as soon help to haul you off a mudflat as laugh at you for pronouncing the letter *r*.

But sailing to Massachusetts entails making plans and plotting courses and buying ice to keep the ice cream warm. It isn't something you do on the spur of impulse. Not like dashing out to the Race to look for larger waves, or sailing up the Connecticut in the hope of getting becalmed. No, careful planning is called for. You need to lay in a goodly supply of chain plates, and inform your next of kin should something untoward—say a fair day—occur. It's most of a day to Cuttyhunk or Westport, and anything has been known to happen in such a stretch of time. People have made and broken marriage engagements; other boats powered by only the wind have been spotted; rectitude has been probed and discovered devoid of much enjoyment; quietude has been apprehended and restrained for examination.

Voyaging over the water is no joke. Some sailors have ventured forth and never returned. A friend of mine once made it through the Cape Cod Canal on a dare, and now is never heard from except at Christmas.

Courvoisier

Spring has arrived.

No, the fact that my clock has been mandated to read an hour fast has little relevance. The fact that I surprised a gay young crocus attempting to vault the dead leaves by the end of the tall stone wall beside my house has little relevance. Nor has the noisy cardinal who seeks a nest mate little, if any, relevance.

"What, then, has?" you query.

Why, only the necessity to begin stripping the varnish from the spars of Herreshoff boats. When the temperature creeps toward forty-five and fifteen knots of wind frisk down the sound, sailboats here in southern Connecticut tend to bite at their mooring lines or climb down out of their cradles. One must remember their fond and innate predisposition for splashing about in the sea. One of these days, I'm sure to find *Moon Wind* has turned herself 'round in her slip to face the cove.

So, here I am, for the umpteenth time, handing down booms and clubs and oars and tillers and spinnaker poles from the racks in the loft of our shop. And scraping and sanding and generally causing a flurry of dust that congregates in my hair and behind my ears. It certainly is no more nuisance than our multitudinous maple flowers that soon will lavish my truck with yellow pollen.

There's a tangible satisfaction in the sheen of eight coats of varnish. A sense of well-being, accomplishment, and a chance to brag are all inherent in every can of finish. Varnish is surely the nectar of the gods. It flows as honey flows from a heated spoon. It hardens to the clarity of ice on a limpid pool. It glows with the benevolence of the sun on a late-spring morning. It dresses the plainest boat in sparkling jewels. It makes you swear you'll never buy a boat with brightwork again.

I tune in the radio and listen to classical music. The announcer puts on Beethoven's Eroica symphony as I wield my keen-edged scraper. Before the first movement ends, I'm down to bare wood and reveling in the shavings. I hope for the calming effect of some Debussy or Massenet by the time I'm ready to lay on the last coat of varnish.

Refinishing portends the boating season, and the weather has become milder, week by week. A good thing, too. My long johns could use a laundering after 414 days of continuous use. And it's time to drain the lovely pink antifreeze from my freshwater system and my holding tank. They now demand that we recycle pink antifreeze and not pollute the sea with it and intoxicate the mackerel.

"But it's perfectly harmless," an outraged fellow boater protested to me. "You can even drink it."

Help yourself, mate. Just hang your snout by this through-hull fitting while I gently pump out my tank.

I recollect a girl I dated who throve on sloe gin fizzes. Maybe those fizzes weren't concocted from sloe berries after all. Maybe they were pink and sweet 'cause the bartender had a boat. Maybe that's why she got excited about this time of year. It's hard to get cozy with someone for whom the high point of the boating season is when we drain our tanks.

I'd venture the opinion that antifreeze is a slowly acquired taste. You need to sip it discreetly; let it roll around your mouth. Its subtle, delicate aftertaste will linger on your tongue. As the evening progresses, you'll find yourself glad to designate a driver. By your fourth or fifth glass, your countenance will glow with renewed benevolence. You will have forgiven your friends their indiscretions, and welcomed your enemies into your open arms.

April could earn a reputation for intemperate antifreeze parties.

But not all of us are partial to this method of recycling. If we aren't to dump our antifreeze in our previous reckless manner and, as many of us would gladly pass if offered a bright pink, presweetened Coolant Cocktail, perhaps we should change our antifreeze altogether.

Courvoisier is another acquired taste. Not only will it prevent your head from freezing, but it has a distinguished lineage and a savory reputation. Just don't tell your Uncle Fromage that you plan to flush his last two bottles of twenty-year-old French brandy down the toilet.

Mariposa

Mariposa

I now hold the patents on the world's first hexamaran. With eighteen masts and just over two square miles of sail area, my prototype vessel, *Mariposa,* can circle the continental shelf in just a tad less than two days, eleven and a quarter minutes.

You may think that a hexamaran would have six parallel hulls. Think again. My six hulls radiate from a common cockpit astern where the navigation ceremonies take place. These consist of burning collected burgees on the altar and watching which way the smoke drifts. When this has been determined, a course can be set in any direction whatever.

Being a hexagram in shape, not only can *Mariposa* sail at over one hundred knots, but she wards off evil spells devised by offshore race committees and disgruntled competitors.

Every sail ever designed should be set simultaneously on one of the eighteen masts. This eliminates the nuisance of changing or shortening sail. You merely put the helm over until the hull flying the sails you want is following the course. This has simplified sailing so much that only four people are required to man this vessel: a chef, a chauffeur, the skipper, and someone to feed the cat. If your cat is self-sufficient and you don't plan to go ashore, you can definitely scratch the skipper from this list.

Just a word about the running rigging. All ninety-two sheets are fed through turning blocks and eventually lead to the computer. Each sheet is secured by a clove hitch to a different key in the keyboard. ~, @, #, $, %, ^, &, *, (,), _, and + control the jibs, and so on and so forth. Just a light tap on the proper key is enough to trim the sail in anything less than force-fourteen breezes. Sheets having a red tracer must be controlled in conjunction with the SHIFT key.

The ENTER key is used for coming about. BACKSPACE is handy to ease into narrow slips. Scrolling, of course, causes the vessel to go to port or starboard, forward or backward. The TAB key is useful for a sudden forward spurt when pursuing mermaids. The DELETE key removes dyspeptic gulls from the mastheads. The function of the HOME key should be obvious.

The design for this innovative vessel came to me one very hot night in the tropics. I'd indulged myself in a heavy meal consisting solely of a gallon of ginger ice cream topped with a syrup composed of triple sec, Kahlúa, and Myers's dark rum. Only my shaman knows how to proportion the ingredients of this syrup. I woke in the night with the room whirling madly about me. This was the inspiration I needed for my central cockpit and radiating hulls.

Although the patent office refused my innovative design at first, they quickly relented. After I took their chief attorney for a moonlight sail and clicked the PAGE DOWN and PAGE UP keys a half dozen times he was convinced. These keys raise and lower the keels of the five hulls not in use. This is important as it greatly reduces the wetted area and keeps the vessel from having too much lee helm. He assured me that nothing even resembling my boat had ever been seen before. I could have told him that.

After all my patentable claims were granted, I took him sailing again—this time for pleasure. He had the helm as we wafted about Bermuda at eighty-four knots. We should have been back in Connecticut before the sun had even selected a yardarm but, impulsively, he reached out and tapped the ESCAPE key.

Rather than tell his wife the awful truth I showed her my photos of mermaids boarding my boat, and intimated he'd suffered a midlife crisis.

Fortunately for all of us who wend this world's waters, all sailors' wives believe whatever they're told.

Electrolysis

We all know about electrolysis. Electric current found in the sea—probably produced during the mating season of electric eels—is responsible for the ionization and redeposition of what we term precious metals—bronze or stainless steel—onto the scales of passing fish. What, then, of the electrolysis that occurs when waves, or even salt spray, pass over a boat when someone is at the helm?

There can be no dissent about which is more precious, the boat or merely the helmsman. Consider the cheapness of human life versus the exorbitant amounts we pay to own and maintain our boats. There can be no doubt that ocean spray ionizes our boats and deposits them, atom by atom, upon us sailors.

People say we grow to assume the attributes of our spouses. I say we grow to assume the attributes of our boats. Portions of our boats, in time, replace those of our bodies. I knew a man who spent the greater part of his life at the wheel of his Tartan 34, sailing down east to Maine every summer with the wind abaft his beam. This fellow has grown a huge billowing thatch of long white hair that has woven itself into the prettiest spinnaker, and the spinnaker sheets are led through the hoops in his ears.

A lady I know spends nearly all her time in a Whitehall pulling boat on Martha's Vineyard. Not only do her fingernails and toenails gleam with eight or ten coats of spar varnish, but her arms and legs have grown to resemble lovely teak rails, and the brightwork continues till it disappears into her sleeves and up her trousers. I'm told by someone who claims to know that her seat is also well varnished. It's said that her shear has so greatly improved that all true sailors turn to watch her every time she rows by, and they say she's grown a small bronze mooring ring in the end of her nose.

Another lady of my acquaintance spends nearly all of her time upon the foredeck. The name WUNG-OUT is painted on her transom. When she spreads her arms before the wind, her mainsail flies from one side, a number two genoa jib flies from the other. If only her sheets weren't so inclined to snag on the foredeck cleat, I'd invite her aboard more often. Last time we were out it was blowing twelve knots but gusting more, and, of course she neglected again to set her preventer. She let the wind get 'round her main for a moment. We jibed so hard she nearly popped her gooseneck out of its socket.

You can tell an old salt not only by his mannerisms but by the way he resembles the boat he sails. When he lifts the cover of his starboard oilskin pocket and takes out some mooring lines and a couple of fenders, you know he's been aboard his boat for a while. Just watch him as he stows his winch handle down inside his port boot. When he's ready to anchor he makes a hawse pipe of his thumb and first finger and the roding snakes out of his sleeve. I knew a skipper who'd fifty fathoms of three-eighths galvanized chain in his trouser pocket. But by then he drew nearly six feet and had an overabundance of lead in his pants.

There's an old man I met who's spent the better portion of his seventy years at sea. His nose always points directly into the wind. It's said that his sloop had a fearsome weather helm. His ears are both triangular and grown so huge that he had two sets of reef points sewn into each. When he takes three turns of double braid 'round his midriff and cranks his arms, he can take up on a jib sheet like nobody's business. He gets along most famously whenever he wets his rail and can make nine knots if his bottom's been recently scraped. They used to race him, when he was younger, from Newport to Bermuda. Now he's used mostly for coasting by a young couple north of Boston. They tell me he spends most of his time in a slip outside of Gloucester, and has the nasty habit of spewing his oakum. But he still shows indications of wanderlust, and they need to keep extra spring lines on him, especially when an offshore breeze is blowing.

Compass Roses

Here I am again at Mystic Seaport, scheduled to sign my books at the gift shop for two hours this bleak, rainy, late-autumn afternoon. Prospects are not of the grandest. A dozen customers walk about, over and back, fondling toy sailboats and Seaport coffee mugs, trying not to think about returning into the rain and lowering twilight.

Only four of my books remain of the bookshop stock—the lees of their quota for this calendar year. In the past hour, no one has done much more than smile at me; no one has stopped to look at or even smell my book—to inhale the salty tang of my memoirs.

So here I sit, drowning my sorrows in coffee and penning my thoughts.

Tomorrow I mean to visit *MoonWind* and fit her with a new cover to exclude snow and ice from her cockpit and most of her new deckhouse. A new green, ripstop nylon tarp—nearly hull color—needs to be draped and secured to stanchion pedestals and pad eyes and about the mast. Tomorrow will be the first day in a week that it won't blow twenty knots with gusts to thirty. Waving a lightweight tarp about in a twenty-knot breeze would be tantamount to flying a personal spinnaker; thirty knots might result in finding myself halfway to Block Island, twenty miles distant, doing six knots between the crests without benefit of my boat.

This means that should I arrive at Great Salt Pond, I'd be reluctant to pick up a mooring—not having brought my dinghy along to row ashore for supper. And coming home close-hauled would be a challenge. Without a mast or boom or even a halyard, beating twenty miles might strain my meager reserve of ingenuity. Just imagine windsurfing without the surfboard.

So, I prefer to fit my boat cover in the calm, then lay below and fire up the stove for a cup of coffee. Then sit at my table and spread a chart before me to plan some future excursion. *I* get excited just unfurling a chart. I always peruse the latest crop of compass roses—those flowers that thrive offshore. That's my primary reason for venturing down the New England coast in *MoonWind*—to pick our beautiful compass roses just as they start to bloom. It amazes me the ongoing market for these exotic flowers—especially among those who aspire to sail but have never consummated their intentions. A bouquet of fragrant compass roses, nay, even a single bloom, has been known to inspire and encourage an inveterate lubber to embark on a life of non-perpendicular pleasure: leaning against the frothy sea, tiller in hand, a stormy petrel nesting within his whiskers.

Ah, for a following breeze and a forward mermaid! For now, I must wait out the winter storms—my love of sailing not so inclusive as to encompass severe discomfort for the sake of proving I can swim with penguins, sleep aboard ice floes, flaunt my frozen beard to inclement Boreas.

I'm but a lazy waterman, fond of fair weather. I excurse in winter merely to appease my darling *MoonWind,* who tires of her frigid slip, and chafes against her numerous halters and spring lines. I would not wish such a sedentary life on any, and *MoonWind* has a free spirit that chafes at restraints.

"Cast off that dock line, lad, and let's away!" she exclaims. "Follow the ebb for uncharted lands—perhaps even those uninhabited islands of Buzzards Bay."

So what can I do? My boat is my mistress, and when she says, "Go!" I go. Admittedly, Buzzards Bay is a long day's sail for *MoonWind,* but we usually camp the first night at Point Judith Pond. And thence, the following morning, to Buzzards Bay, where hospitable harbors abound and the sailing delights, and an island beckons at the close of each rigorous day. There are but too few seasons in the midst of life, and too few days to cleave these responsive waters.

And thus I admonish each of you: to follow your feet to the pier where *Moon Wind* bides; to purchase a bouquet of freshly picked compass roses from my mermaid and display it conspicuously in a crystal vase, that your aspirations and inclinations neither wilt nor remain becalmed; and to speak encouraging words to your shivering boat this frore but terminable winter.

The Art of Not Quite Going Aground

If you've never gone aground, don't worry. Opportunities abound within a mile of where your sailboat swings wistfully on her mooring or strains against her spring lines at the pier. If you're bashful about undertaking a project like this yourself, just entrust the helm to your cousin Elmer, who's always wanted to learn how to sail, and show him that estuary where the blue crabs get *this big*. To do it properly, wait until it's high tide. You do want a story to tell around the fireplace this Christmas, don't you? And you do want a story that can't be told in a measly half hour, right? By the time you're done describing how you kedged your anchor by wading through slimy eelgrass in the nude, you're sure to have your choice of any seat beside the fire.

I suppose you're going to ask me whether I've ever gone aground. Personally, I don't see how that's any business of yours. I'm here to give advice. As everyone knows, those without experience are always first in line when it comes to offering their opinions on anything whatsoever. That's why I took up writing in the first place.

Before I go too much farther, I need to explain to any of you who are bluewater sailors that this is what the rest of us do on our weekends. Rather than cross the North Atlantic on Saturday afternoon, we merely sail for a few hours, then look for a handy mudflat to settle on for the evening. I've done a little bluewater sailing, and the one thing I noticed was the difficulty in preparing a truly gourmet meal when heeled sixty degrees.

Even anchored, chopping onions can be a challenge when *Sea Puss* bucks on her halter. Much as you may be tempted to add a finger to the marinara sauce, you know your vegetarian daughter is bound to complain about it. It's only when you're snuggled rather firmly into the mud that you don't have to worry about the cutting board sliding into

90

the bilge. Catamarans, of course, were specifically designed by a four-star chef to rest on the bottom in the interests of haute cuisine. The fact that they can be sailed is only of secondary importance.

Just a couple of weeks ago, I took *Moon Wind* up the Mystic River. The mouth of the harbor is carefully marked by several relevant aids to navigation, one of which consists of a pole jammed among the ever-invisible rocks on Ram Island Shoals. Ram Island Shoals are one temptation I haven't succumbed to, yet. Between the west entrance to Mystic Harbor and Ram Island, there's loads and loads of water: nearly enough to fill that pretty boat of yours to the brim as she sits on the bottom among some neighborly rocks. If you'd like to enjoy the dry portion of Ram Island, follow the street signs and drive your boat to the easterly shore and park between the stripes in the scenic cove.

Once you get into Mystic Harbor, channel markers abound. There's a goodly jog in the channel 'round Sixpenny Island just above Noank. You can follow the two-fathom-deep channel that skirts the acres and acres of mooring field or, to save at least a quarter mile, take your chance and cut through them. Having a chart can prove a welcome distraction. If you scrutinize it for more than five minutes at once, the chances of your going aground improve by 80 percent.

Ogling lovely boats on their moorings is a time-honored means to avoid scraping the bottom. As long as a boat on a nearby mooring draws as much as yours does, how can you possibly go aground? Centerboard boats, of course, draw nearly nothing. I wonder if this is one, here?

Though *Moon Wind* draws only four feet, she happens to be inquisitive, and I've found myself, more than once or twice, scaring the quahogs while I admired moored boats. My chart declares that the far side of the mooring field in Mystic Harbor has about five feet of water at mean low tide. A lot of the art of going aground revolves around answering, just how low and how mean? If you've recently spent huge wads of money having your bottom painted, you might want to stick to the channel.

To the east of Ram Island, beyond that mooring field, just beyond that area where no one moors except for a few small skiffs, lies the other entrance to Mystic Harbor. Of course there's a well-marked channel to that deep water just inboard of Ram Island. All you need to figure out is whether to leave those red things to port or to starboard. I suppose it depends on whether you think you're readily, rightly returning, and if you aren't, what other plans did you have for this afternoon? Besides recollecting whether you paid that overdue premium on your tow insurance.

Even if you behave yourself and follow the channel up the Mystic River, you can always run aground by Six Penny Island. It's a perfect place to let your children run around and scare the fiddler crabs. Or you can truly embarrass yourself by getting hung up off Mystic Seaport where thousands of people can watch you and applaud.

First, of course, you need to get by both bridges. Our railroad trestle caters to Amtrak, and sports a clever digital sign that reads: BRIDGE WILL OPEN AGAIN IN BLANK, BLANK MINUTES. But the only digits I've ever seen it register were both zeros. These are your choices: You can call the bridge tender on channel 13 and offer to buy him roses; wait until the express goes by and he swings the span on his own; or push very hard on the bridge with your mast until it opens enough to let you through.

Between this swing bridge and the bascule bridge that allows the two halves of Mystic to visit each other, there aren't many opportunities to run your boat aground. Piers and marinas and slips crowd either shore. The bascule bridge has a sign informing the far of sight that it opens only at forty minutes past the hour all "boating season," and only by request November through April. This request should be pinned to a twenty-pound turkey and left in the bridge tender's cabin by mid-November.

Protocol states that during boating season (whenever that is) you get in line either side of this bridge and mark time till the bridge tender wakes from his nap. If you have a motor, this is a good time to see if it really works. If your motor won't start, tie a long piece of line to it and lower it over the side till it rests on the bottom. A scope of only three to one will allow you to step ashore to buy some ice cream while you're waiting.

Above the bridge, the Mystic River widens and widens and widens. A mile upstream, it spreads a half mile across. Of course, there are channel markers a part of the way—just past Mystic Seaport. The channel here boasts over eight feet of water. The rest of the river is unencumbered by markers, moorings, rocks, or other hazards to navigation. The only things you need to avoid are the egrets and herons stalking their lunch alongside. If you consult your chart you'll find the upriver soundings appropriate for kayaks. If you have a small twin-hulled or twin-keeled boat, you can sneak up there at the height of the tide and spend your summer settling into the mud. The view alone is worthwhile, and we generally get some really high tides around the Equinox.

When I was up here, two weeks ago, showing one of my publishers the Seaport, I navigated strictly through intuition. Just beyond the last of the channel markers, three large sloops swung on their mooring pendants. Outboard of the green channel marker, there isn't quite water enough to drown a flounder. I hugged the shore as close as I dared, mindful that the tide had just begun making. When my crew began to pick violets from the bank I began to get nervous. Above the marker and twenty yards shy of the first big sloop, I put the helm down, hard. *MoonWind* bucked just a little bit, kicked up her heels, and a cloud of mud roiled briefly in her wake. She came about within the channel and trotted back by the Seaport toward the bridge.

And that's the closest I've come to running aground so far this season. But then, it's only August.

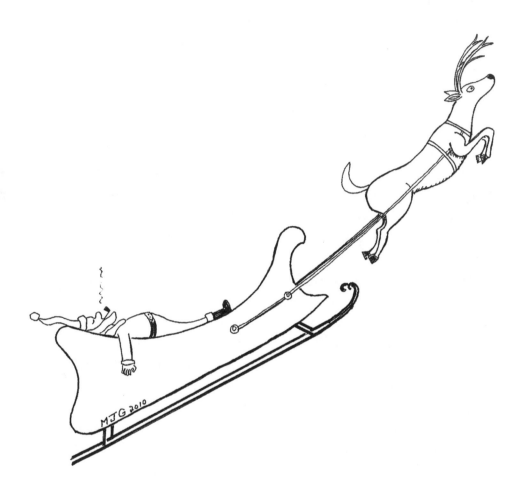

Half-past Christmas

30 December 2009

The year has unwound so far I can see the spool. Not many chances remain to sail this year but, at ten degrees above nothing, I'm little inclined to climb aboard and cast off my mooring lines this lovely morning.

Yesterday I went to the boatyard to check on poor frozen *Moon Wind* and the Whitehall in their slip. It was fifteen degrees, and the northwest wind howled down Fishers Island Sound at thirty, gusting to forty. Within the marina, sheltered on three sides, its power was much diminished. Due to our recent temperate weather, the water remained several balmy degrees above thirty-two, and the two inches of water in my Whitehall sloshed about, only a skim of ice upon its surface.

I retrieved a two-quart paint pot from *Moon Wind*'s locker, unclipped the Whitehall's after tether, pulled her to the pier, and bailed her dry. I ducked beneath the tarpaulin covering *Moon Wind*'s cockpit, tipped her outboard into the drink, and pushed the starter button. She fired on the second push and roared and spewed out water. I let her roar as I snugged three or four of the cords securing the tarp. After several minutes, the motor warmed, the choke disengaged, the motor hummed a chantey of harbor prowling.

I lay below and checked my bilge and sniffed for signs of mildew. I liberated my GPS, fetched my boating shoes, and tripped up the pier to stow them in my truck. I returned and took up on my windward spring lines, turned off my motor, and tucked her in for the week. I secured my main hatch, checked my chafing gear, and kissed *Moon Wind* good-bye.

From the end of the pier, I could see five-footers galloping down the sound. The ample spindrift turned to frozen mist above the water—"sea smoke" we call it hereabouts—and I shuddered to think of it coming over my bow while under way. The windchill hovered at five below, and the harbor seals had icicles in their whiskers. Not a good day to take a relaxing sail.

More a day to finish stacking my stove wood by the kitchen door. More a day to debate the virtues of a second cup of coffee. More a day to reminisce, to write, to read, to plan.

And so I write this, and stoke the fire, and cycle laundry, and keep the Pusslets amused. I need to research the histories of the fifty landmarks making up my next book. I need to pick up my journals and cards at consignment shops that plan to close for the winter. I need to plan what further repairs are necessary to assuage *MoonWind*'s limitless appetite for manual labor. *My* manual labor.

Projects include partitioning the two lockers beneath my settees, that I may stow more gear without its falling into the bilge. And finishing off an auxiliary locker astern for stowing a second rode and chain. I already have a Danforth clamped to my taffrail. I need to deploy it quickly astern from the cockpit when single-handing. I can also take the rode forward and set two anchors from the bow. I need to fabricate a new hatch cover for my forward settee. I need to glass in my battery so it can't go waltzing about. I need to rip up and recore my deck, rebed my lifeline stanchion pedestals, apply new nonskid to the cockpit and the deck. I need to replace my starboard lifeline. I need to replace the hinges on my cockpit locker. I need to fill old screw holes in my main salon with gel coat and blend them in. I need to replace my teak porthole surrounds. I need to hang some new curtains.

One of these days, everything may be accomplished. Well, almost everything. Then I can bask in smug assurance that I'm prepared for any eventuality. Although I've taken basic courses in basking, I need to improve my technique. I must appear quite lackadaisical, unconcerned, and aloof while I lounge about my cockpit at the marina.

That, of course, is the only reason to have a slip instead of merely a mooring: exposure to more boaters. On a sultry day when the wind refuses to blow, I can laze about *MoonWind*'s cockpit and assure other sailors stalking the pier I've nothing at all to do. Of course, being sailors, their need to be told some lies is quite insatiable, and the only reason I ever get anything published.

WEST COVE—NOANK

The Seahorse, Noank, Connecticut

"And the waters prevailed . . ." —Genesis

Verisimilitude

This vigorous morning growls in my massive, fieldstone chimney. The maple logs roar back. Tired of their incessant debate, I close the door on both of them and rumble down to the boatyard.

Twenty knots ruffle Fishers Island Sound. Some of the ruffles stand as tall as I do. Not a good day to play intrepid mariner on my twenty-six-foot sloop. *MoonWind* strains at her doubled-up mooring lines. Chilly water sloshes the finger pier. The sloop in the slip upwind of me, *Sea Biscuit,* bucks on her halter and shakes her salty mane.

This weekend, I presumed, would be apt for sailing. This Sunday, indeed, proves a day of abundant sun. And abundant wind. I square away *MoonWind,* uncover her mainsail, and hoist it at the slip. *Moon-Wind* thinks I mean her to sail, and does her best to clamber over the pier.

"Not yet, my lass," I tell her as I slack the sheet some more. "I need to shorten your sail a bit before we take you out."

I roller reef the snapping mainsail down to the bottom batten, then douse it and secure it with two bungees. I prime the motor and push the starter button. The motor wakes, yawns once, and purrs contentedly. I scratch her ears and tell her what a good girl she is. A little encouragement goes a long way with motors.

My crew shows up and begins to grump about some frivolous waves he detects cavorting about the sound. Where else would he expect a wave to cavort?

At his insistence, I flip on my VHF. Twenty knots, gusting to twenty-eight, says the simulated, nearly human, voice. Simulated voices start me thinking: a precarious venture even on mild days. I try to imagine a totally engineered voice: sans tongue, sans mouth, sans teeth, sans vocal cords. My imagination reels.

Think of it, I say to myself: a voice without a body. Seems there'd be a bigger market for bodies without voices. Many of us would gleefully part with our wallets for such a spouse. All *I* desire is to have this voice lie to my crew concerning the weather.

Why can't it say that the wind blows only ten knots? That the chaos beyond the breakwater is simply one of J. M. Turner's more frenetic seascapes? *I've* been lied to before. *I* survived it.

My crew has little interest in mere survival. He wants a relaxing sail. To sail when the small craft warning tatters loudly at Morgan Point apparently disqualifies as relaxing. I try to tempt him with promises of adventure, thrills, and drowning. He responds with an urge to visit a distant marine consignment shop. He tells me his life has taken a turn for the better. He explains to me that he's much too young to drown.

"You're fifty years old," I tell him. "Why would anyone want to live longer than that?"

"Come on," he says. "I'll drive."

I snap the sail cover over the mainsail. I turn my motor off. I tell her what a good girl she's been and tip her out of the water. I secure my forward hatch. I never got to hanking on a jib. Maybe I'll find a storm jib at the marine consignment shop. I replace my drop boards, slide my main hatch closed, cover my bulkhead compass. I kiss *Moon-Wind* good-bye. My crew turns up his collar.

"It's blowing a little harder, now," he says.

"The problem is," I remonstrate, "your younger generation has no . . ."

"Why don't you go out by yourself?" he counters.

"Do you think they might have a storm jib at this place we're going?" I ask him.

"Don't forget your lunch," he says. "We can park at the point and eat our lunch in the car and watch the sea."

The way it's blowing, I figure I can hold my sandwich out the car window in between bites and let the spray nearly ruin it. Real men *never* leave the helm to eat lunch.

Besides—my writing thrives on verisimilitude.

Noank Baptist Church

Christmas Eve Day

Christmas once again and the twilit dawn reveals frost. The houseful of family about me revels in slumber. The Pusslets are outside worshipping at the bird feeder. At least there is nothing hypocritical about their devotions: A more simplistic creed cannot be imagined.

Went to the lobster pound yesterday with Ethan and Marya and found eight lobsters eager for martyrdom.

"Heaven awaits," we told them, and they jumped in the back of my truck and refused to come out. May a quick and delicious death with lots of melted butter await us all.

After that we drove to the boatyard and visited with *MoonWind*, sulking in her slip. All alone at the end of the pier behind our empty shop, she wondered at her isolation. The electricity to pier A and the shop has been turned off preparatory to demolishing our old boat shop building.

I started *MoonWind*'s motor and prepared to move her to a vacant slip over on pier B. The wind was out of the west, so we warped *Moon-Wind* downwind across the double slip and eased her toward the channel. I backed her into the stream and motored slowly to her new berth. But I hadn't noticed the spring line someone had left attached to the cleats. Perhaps this dock had a tenant. Just to be sure I backed her out a second time. This time was even easier as the wind was totally blocked by a larger sloop with a heavy, canvas enclosure.

I found a slip at pier C and settled in. Adjusted the lines and fenders, squared her away, tucked her in, wished her a Merry Christmas, and departed.

Ethan revealed an idea he had of spending summers aboard a sloop with his family. With a wireless Internet connection he can work anywhere. As Alicia teaches she has the summers off. They poked around a few boats. She didn't think she could manage on anything less than a thirty-three-footer. Anything they could afford would require extensive work. It can be daunting to undertake such projects when you haven't any experience.

I suggested he spend an occasional week aboard *Moon Wind,* learning the ropes. He thought that would prove a reasonable compromise for the present though he and his wife are too tall for *Moon Wind's* cabin. Nonetheless, he needs to practice messing about with anchoring, docking, maneuvering in tight spaces. On blowy days handling boats can be tricky, and single-handing in adverse conditions demands one's utmost attention. All the expedients of warping need be considered, and forethought, lines and fenders, and allowance for set and drift all factored in. One doesn't make friends by bouncing off other boats.

Though it wasn't that windy I appreciated having extra hands while moving *Moon Wind.* Getting both bow and stern secured before the wind can swing them about takes not only forethought, but perfect execution. One may need to leap to the pier and secure two lines within seconds. One mustn't approach the slip too quickly. The moments spent in backing down are moments the wind can shove your boat around. One mustn't approach the slip too slowly, either, for just the same reason. You need to point into the wind whenever possible; when it's blowy you may want to back into the wind. In either case allow for drift as soon as you head off. As with most undertakings of significance, timing is everything.

Winter is arrived but continues unseasonably mild. I need to go sailing before it reverts to normal. Sitting before the fire induces dreams. Riding the wind is reward for being alive.

The Whitehall

Finally hauled my Whitehall pulling boat yesterday. She's been tethered in my summer slip behind our old shop that isn't there anymore. Every other boat was moved when they turned the power off two months ago preparatory to dismantling the building. I moved *Moon-Wind* but left my Whitehall, meaning to take her home.

Last week we had an ice storm. The Whitehall collected about three inches of precipitation and rendered it solid ice. As the temperature has scarcely made it to freezing this past month, and promised to continue, I decided it was time to leave my swivel chair and act.

I had checked my friend's Able 20 after the ice storm. His cockpit drains had frozen solid and several inches of ice had usurped his cockpit. The two of us went down to the yard on Sunday to solve our problems.

He wanted to row my Whitehall the two hundred yards to the ramp. He's wanted to row her ever since I bought her three years ago. She's a heavy boat—well over a hundred pounds—but she tracks very well and her weight provides her momentum. Her seven-and-a-half-foot spruce oars are perfect for her eleven, six length and nearly four-foot beam. Unfortunately, the adjustable footrest was embedded in the ice. Aside from that and the extra weight, he had an enjoyable row.

Part of the water around the ramp was frozen, but he edged her up to the pier. I held her as he climbed out. Then we hauled her onto the ramp and attempted, unsuccessfully, to lift her into my truck. Amazing how much thirty gallons of frozen water is attracted to the earth. And how much it refuses bailing.

I looked behind my seat and, amid the confusion of tools and towels and gloves and jumper cables, found a hard rubber mallet. Just the thing to convince that troublesome ice to abandon ship. We tossed out pounds and pounds of it. Then we hoisted the Whitehall up and secured her for the ride.

In my driveway we laid her upside down across two horses. I scrubbed the slime from her bottom, sluiced her down, gave her a pillow and blanket, and tucked her in. I would have read her a story, but she was already sound asleep.

We returned to the boatyard and dealt with his Able 20. He turned on his portable heater and discovered it didn't work. We drove to the local heater store and purchased a new one and twenty pounds of rock salt. We debated whether this latter could harm the boat, and decided it might corrode metal and would probably deteriorate fabric and paint. As his drains are PVC and his cockpit, gel coat, we dumped several pounds of salt on top of his iceberg. The new heater went down below, aimed at the frozen drains. The effect of the salt was immediate and gratifying. We replaced a dock line forward and buttoned up his boat.

MoonWind had little ice in her. My drains led out the transom without any hoses. A partial puddle of ice was all that remained. However, my companionway sliding hatch was frozen solid. The sleet had built up on the forward side an inch thick. As I'd varnished my hatch slides this fall, I wasn't eager to pile rock salt on them. Perhaps today I'll try some mallet therapy.

My outboard motor started right up. It gasped a few times while I pumped the primer bulb, then smoothed out. The automatic choke worked well—in a couple of minutes she settled right down as gratified as any contented kitten. I ran her ten minutes, then turned her off and tipped her out of the water. I scrubbed the slime from her housing and prop and left her out of the water. The zinc looked intact. It's important to take precautions against electrolysis: We don't encourage our mummichogs to sport aluminum scales.

The ocean declined, for once, to assault the shore. The temperature clawed past the freezing mark. A delightful day of sun and sparkling water. Several people messed about on their boats at the finger piers: started their engines; scraped away ice; secured their tarpaulins; visualized lilacs and daffodils.

Outboard Blues

Moon Wind's outboard motor acted a bit cranky on Sunday when we were out—hesitant and tentative: same as I act when someone insists I move more quickly or act more responsively or responsibly or whatever that word is.

Yesterday I went down to the pier after work armed with my bright orange toolbox, determined not to go home until that motor arched its back and purred. Long about nightfall I got so hungry I was chewing on the spare fuel hose that I keep for such emergencies.

First I removed my six-gallon, portable fuel tank and dumped the old gas into my truck's tank. My truck seems quite impervious to having a couple of gallons of stale gas mixed in with a half tank. At least she never complains the way my outboard does.

I strapped my tank back in its compartment and gave it a long drink of fresh fuel with stabilizer. I'm tempted to try a little stabilizer myself. Might help me keep my footing when I'm surfing through heavy chop.

Then I changed the water separator cartridge. I've mounted the casing so I can slip a gallon plastic bucket beneath it. Off with the old, on with the new. Then prime the fuel system and . . . well, what I forgot was, all of that air in the filter casing has to go somewhere when you squeeze the primer bulb. There just isn't room in the carburetor for most of it.

At first, I thought that the new filter casing wasn't seated properly—that I was sucking air past its seal—so I kept tightening it, without seeing any improvement. Then I put back the old casing, after dumping the water and filth from it. Still no success. After removing the primer bulb and testing it with a spare length of hose, then replacing it, then removing it and replacing it with my spare bulb, still without being able to prime the system, it suddenly occurred to me that I needed to bleed all that air, or else fill the filter case with fuel.

Bleeding the line appeared the less messy choice. I popped the line off the motor, depressed the check valve with a little screwdriver, and pumped the bulb a few times. Guess what? Fuel began to emerge from the fuel line. Revelations of my stupidity never cease to amaze me. Wasting forty minutes on a five-minute project never fails to have its effect. Seems as though I'd had this problem before and solved it the same way. Maybe the little gray cells need to be sent out and be re-conditioned. Can't remember where I sent them the last time . . .

I then changed the plugs after first checking the gaps with my trusty feeler gauge. I pushed the starter button and, Bingo! She started right up, ran for three minutes, sputtered and died. Hmmm. Must be time for supper.

Before I quit I removed the little in-line fuel filter and took it with me. Perhaps a fresh one will solve my woes. Or at least my motor's woes. On my way to the head to wash up I encountered my local mechanic messing about in his shop. Just back-flush that little filter with some carb cleaner, he told me, then run the whatsis out of the motor for an hour. Maybe increase the idle speed a bit. If that doesn't work he'll take it into his shop and teach it some manners.

It's time I made a serious effort to square away *Moon Wind's* troubles. A month from today I'm supposed to go onto my mooring. Once on a mooring, excessive pitching makes repairs more difficult. Tools have to be battery-powered. Fresh water for cleaning up is hard to come by. The marina frowns on running a quarter mile of hose from the ultimate pier, over the breakwater, and through the mooring field. Not sure why. Probably interferes with the cormorants chasing mummichogs for their breakfast.

We always look out for our cormorants hereabouts. *Our* cormorants never shit on our boats. They only chase the hapless mummichogs about the harbor, then suddenly broach alongside to show you proudly what they've caught.

Yesterday a pair of swans came by while I was hanging over my transom. They hadn't a thing to show me. I'd just attempted to prime the motor for the 114th time.

"Get a job," I growled.

Heads in the air, they swam to pier C and condescended to be admired by the couple on the trawler. They were just in time for hors d'oeuvres.

Spring Cleaning

Spring has arrived, abruptly, urgently, gracefully, and at last. Although there is frost at daybreak, earth embraces the gracious sun as a lover. From the heat of their love, their progeny, the daffodils and narcissi, lift their lovely young faces to the morning.

Today I should have spread my single wing and sailed away. The welding shop has not repaired my gooseneck slide, and *Moon Wind* has but her jib to wave at the wind. Should have, but I chose instead to catch up on yearly maintenance before I depart my winter slip for my mooring.

The weather has been so cold that very few boats are in the water. At forty degrees with a stout, damp breeze, few mariners uncover their boats, let alone wax and buff them or paint their bottoms. This weekend it soared to seventy. Vehicles crowded every vacancy left behind by launched boats. I parked my truck at our shop across the road.

First thing I did was turn *Moon Wind* around so her transom would face the pier. As no one yet shares my slip, and the breeze was gentle, I simply shifted lines and fenders, hauled on her stern and slacked her bow, and let the breeze coax her about. At only forty-five hundred pounds, *Moon Wind* needs but a leash and the merest encouragement to obey. After I'd secured her I could reach the trim tab of my outboard motor to change the anode.

Next, I removed my hand pump that pumps waste overboard, and discovered seepage around the diaphragm gasket. No wonder the vee berth smelled like a thunder mug. While I was at it I removed the hose and elbow between the pump and the through-hull fitting. Then I had to clean up the mess I'd made. Hanging from the forward hatch with my ears in the bilge was so much fun I resolved to attack the mildew that lurks in my cockpit. Once you're filthy why not revel in it? On with the rubber gloves, break out the bleach, rig the hose, and show that mildew who's the boss around here. Domination—that's all we want.

Moon Wind has a separated cockpit; the aftermost two feet are partitioned off at the height of the cockpit lockers. On either side, aft, is an open-faced compartment that houses a six-gallon fuel tank. I removed the covers and fuel tanks and scrubbed them. Soon as I let the daylight in, the accumulated compost in those compartments warmed up. Obscene and unmentionable things began to sprout. I needed a permit from the Department of Agriculture before I commenced the harvest. After I scythed down the mildew, I scrubbed the entire cockpit, the coamings, and the deck. Only then was I allowed to play with the hose.

Spraying water proved so much fun that I flushed the antifreeze out of the water tank. Then I reconnected the pump and filter, filled the tank, and found fresh water streaming into my sink. I was just in time to wash my hands before the EPA could cordon them off with yellow tape.

I also refastened the mounting clips to the newly varnished companionway ladder and put that back into place. Swinging into the cabin by the topping lift has its attractions, especially if you remember to remove the drop boards first. But, last time I tried it, I managed to wedge myself in the magazine rack where there was nothing worth reading save a two-year-old *New Yorker*. What a treat to have a ladder with brand-new nonskid treads and glistening wood!

At the shop, I completed ventilating the door to my hanging locker with a one-inch hole saw, sanded all the sharp edges of twenty-six holes, and painted all the raw surfaces with primer.

In the midst of all this, I managed to find the time for a lengthy jaw with a couple of sailors and remembered to eat the peanut butter and homemade elderberry jelly sandwich I'd brought along for the ride.

Despite the lovely weather scarcely any mariners ventured out. I wonder if they rather prefer the cleaning and socializing to the sailing. Odd how reluctant we all can be when it comes to cleaning house. But make us pay thousands of dollars for the privilege of storing our boats in the sea, and watch us wield sponge and mop, scrub and scour, polish the bronze, until we convince ourselves that it's safe to sail.

Latham—Chester Store, Noank Historical Society

Putting Her on Her Mooring

Sunday I walked down the pier to *Moon Wind* with my tools and my lunch, prepared to install two small vents in my cockpit. The skipper of a brand-new powerboat across the way hailed me.

"I think you're in my slip," he chuckled. "But it doesn't matter."

We spent a half hour swapping yarns and I promised to move my boat on Monday morning. The weather has been so wretched this spring that half the slips are empty, but I should have been on my mooring a month ago. I've taken advantage of the time to get some projects done: install a solar-powered vent, rebuild a pump, replace a drain, repair my boom.

Improving the circulation in my boat has taken priority. Sunday I bored two four-inch holes in my aftermost bulkhead, above my fuel tanks. There's a gap of several inches between this bulkhead and my transom. Now I have an access port to reach the nuts securing my two aft chain plates, two of my taffrail stanchions, the two chocks on my quarters, and the wiring for my stern running light. All of these things were assembled on the deck and hull before they were bonded together, and have been totally inaccessible.

After checking all the above, I mounted small stainless vents to cover the holes I'd made, but sealed them with silicone so I can easily remove them. Now I have another project: to find two larger chocks to replace the pair I have. I finished the afternoon by grinding out digs and cracks in my fiberglass sole and filling them with epoxy. Now I'm ready to glue down nonskid matting on my sole. There's nothing more disconcerting than sliding about the galley waving a skillet of burning onions every time someone's wake disturbs your anchorage.

Monday morning I loaded my yellow kayak in my truck and headed for Noank. The Whitehall is presently in my garage awaiting

112

transom repairs, and launch service at our boatyard doesn't begin until the end of the month. I found that my kayak fits perfectly between the shrouds and the deckhouse. I also discovered how tipsy it is when you try to climb down into it from on board.

I disconnected my shore power, coiled my hose, filled my gas tank, and brought my charts on board. The sea was dead calm. I motored out and found my mooring, rigged my chafing gear, coiled and stowed my mooring lines, and tossed the kayak over the side. I haven't a boarding ladder. That's another priority. I need to decide whether to find a ladder that merely hooks over my rail or whether to interrupt my lifeline and install new stanchions to form a gate, then secure a folding ladder to my rail. Although more work, this option provides a much steadier means of ascent.

I sat on the deck, dangled my legs over the side, ducked beneath the lifeline, and stepped down into the kayak. At this point, the kayak leaned over to inspect the mushroom anchor. Remember all those illustrations depicting center of gravity versus center of buoyancy? The ones that explain what happens when your sailboat gets knocked down? Yep. When your feet are in the kayak, which is heeled fifty degrees, and your body is over the harbor, and your fingers are clutching desperately at the toe rail of your sloop, things appear a bit grim. If not exactly grim, at least portentously damp. When I managed to reach a standing position in the kayak I was facing the stern. To turn around and sit down in something that's auditioning for an act at Barnum & Bailey proves your agility.

When I finally shoved off, I had a delightful paddle through the mooring field. As yet there are but a half dozen boats on their moorings. But the weather has taken a rapid turn for the better, and the boatyard is launching boats at a furious pace. While I was securing *MoonWind* the boatyard skiff brought out two sailboats, rafted together, and got them settled in for the summer season.

One hundred fifty boats will be moored here soon. Another four hundred are housed in slips. Fewer than one hundred winter wet. Another hundred are small enough for their owners to launch themselves. That leaves a mere 350 boats for the yard to launch in two or three months.

Yesterday I watched an owner chasing his boat, a wet paintbrush in his hand. As the tractor never exceeded eight miles per hour, and the lift slip was a quarter mile away, he managed to get some bottom paint on his rudder just in time.

Paula's Birthday

Took Paula sailing yesterday, but we didn't get under way until after lunch. As the Whitehall hadn't recovered from her sixth and a half coat of varnish, we walked out the pier where the dinghies reside and waited for the launch. To while the time I strolled out pier F to look for *Aurora*. She wasn't in her slip. A white-haired skipper squared away his sloop. I inquired after my friend.

"He's not returning," he told me. "Living aboard in the Chesapeake and consulting from his cabin. Said he'd be headin' for Nova Scotia later on this summer. Probably stop here long enough to tie up and wash off some salt."

This was news: my web master at large in his Island Packet.

We took the launch out to *Moon Wind*. First thing I did was affix a floating whip to one of the two mooring pendants. At the top of the whip I tied a yard of shocking pink survey ribbon. Now I can claim my mooring is haut couture.

In the mooring field, the wind seemed more than adequate. I refrained from bending on a jib until I knew more of the weather. My mate requested we maintain perpendicularity. Actually, Paula never employs long words like that. What she actually said was, "I'd like a relaxing sail." We motored away from the mooring, she at the helm while I went forward to remove the stops, secure the lazy jacks, and raise the main.

Suddenly, *bump* went *Moon Wind*.

"What was that?" I wondered.

"A rock," said Paula.

"There aren't rocks here," I said.

"There are now," she responded.

This at the flood, no less. I quickly tossed my ball cap over the side to mark the spot. I hoisted the main and took back the helm, keeping her close to the wind and against the tide. I planned to work upwind and keep the tide to bring us home should the breeze fail.

Well, it never failed completely. Nor did it blow completely. The tide set us easterly quicker than I could beat westerly. I mentioned setting a jib, but Paula preferred we continue lazing along. At least we had steerageway. The sun, which shone all morning, decided to take a little nap in the clouds. By the time we reached the Clumps by Fishers Island we'd been set a mile and lay opposite Ram Island. When I came about I could barely buck the tide. After a half hour of counting the bubbles alongside I started the motor and headed home to West Cove.

At the mouth of the Mystic River the schooner *Argeia* struggled for steerageway. She'd only her jib and mainsail set and could have doubled her sail area with the foresail and forestaysail, but chose instead to drop her jib and to motor. The main she kept up for appearance's sake as her cargo consisted of sightseers. After I passed her I fell off the wind, killed my motor, and reached the last half mile to our mooring field.

"Now let's look for pink ribbon," I said. "Should be right about . . . there."

When we came within a hundred yards, we spotted it. I spilled some wind and crept discreetly closer. Paula brandished the boat hook in the eyes. I put the helm down and drifted up to our buoy. Almost. *MoonWind* decided to stop about eight feet shy. The boathook is six feet long. Paula's reach is exactly twenty-three inches. The breeze began to shove our bow away.

I fell off the wind and slacked the main and proceeded to caracole *MoonWind* among the fleet. I jibed her briskly about a moored sloop whose skipper lazed aboard.

"Showing off," he chuckled.

I'm not sure what he referred to: I'm sure I missed his bowsprit by at least a foot. I hardened up astern of him, patted his boat on her transom, beat another hundred yards, tacked between two bouncing boats, and trampled my mooring buoy under foot. I suppose I could have employed my motor but it didn't seem sporting somehow.

After we squared away *Moon Wind,* we called the launch. Six sailors and two dogs were going ashore. One dog, a young chocolate Lab, is an avid sailor. The other, a beautiful, brindled boxer-Labrador mix, slumped disconsolately on the deck in his stiff new life preserver.

"Today was his first day aboard," his owners told us. "We stayed on the mooring to let him get acclimated."

The chocolate Lab bounced and cavorted about the launch and sought out instant attention with her nose. The launch driver gave her a biscuit.

"You're such a good girl," he told her.

She couldn't have agreed with him more.

Arrghhh!

At least went daysailing this week. Tuesday took Ethan and Alicia out for the afternoon. Jasper, age five, insisted he did not want to go. He'd been last year and the year before and was timid when confronted by so much water. Same as Saturday night when facing his bath. As usual, we consoled him but didn't leave him behind.

"I don't like it, when are we going back?" grows repetitious.

Fortunately, he is fond of pirates just now.

"Arrrgh!" he hollers. "Avast!"

He spends his every spare moment honing his cutlass.

Any sort of books or regalia having to do with buccaneers is eagerly assimilated. He reads quite well, and devotes many hours to books on robbery, mayhem, and sailing ships. Ships? He had called my boat a ship. This led to the revelation that a pirate needs to know how to steer a ship. Once we arrived at the Spanish Main he was at the helm, reading the compass and holding a steady course, and telling his parents, lolling on the foredeck, how well he was doing steering Grandpa's "ship."

The breeze was a delicious eight knots and steady for a change. The sky was bright, the water was wet, and the helmsman had the time of his life for half a swashbuckled hour. Late in the voyage we boarded and plundered the lobster pound and celebrated in true piratical splendor.

Saturday, went out for a couple of hours with Paula. Who doesn't care all that much for buccaneering. Eight to ten knots, said my forecasters on the Internet. They neglected to mention the frequent gusts to twenty. I should have taken a reef at the mooring, but it didn't look very rough in Fishers Island Sound. It wasn't. Until the tide changed and a nasty chop set in. Bouncing over the chop while heeled over thirty degrees is not Paula's honeyed cup of herbal tea. And when it's puffy it's difficult to eat your sandwich without the peppers jumping overboard.

A couple of lumpy hours proved more than enough. We went home, packed a hamper, and spent the evening in the park with four thousand other people, listening to the local chorale sing nostalgic Broadway show tunes. I found it difficult to pay attention with such a small sea running. Settled back with one leg draped over the tiller and nodded off.

Sunday, went out alone to the mooring and prepared for a hearty sail. Breeze was ten to fifteen knots and *MoonWind* champed at her halter, raring to run. I squared her away, then thought about my nearly full holding tank. I raised the pump-out boat on 68. Yes, he could be there sometime that afternoon. Could he pump the boat tomorrow when I wasn't aboard? No, he answered. I supposed I would wait until he came as my holding tank would soon be sprouting roses. I neglected to ask how soon he'd be arriving.

Now I know better. I started one project then went on to another. The pump-out boat worked its laborious, fragrant way through Mystic Harbor. At three o'clock I overheard someone from our marina asking his whereabouts. He'd be there in an hour and a half I heard him respond. Four thirty! So much for any sailing that afternoon. I tuned in a baseball game and got out the sandpaper. A boat owner's work is never done.

At half past five the pump-out boat came steaming up the channel. He went to the pier and found the boat that had called him. It was now the top of the sixth and the bases were loaded. So was my holding tank. I made a cautious contribution and waited for relief. So did the losing pitcher. We both received relief but his arrived first.

I'd gotten to my mooring via the launch. Her hours abruptly end at seven o'clock. At half past six I called the pump-out boat. He'd made it as far as pier F. Other skippers had flagged him down, as was their right. This pump-out boat is run by the town as a public service, free

119

of charge. You tip the young man or woman who runs it as you see fit. The fitness of my sight was quickly dimming.

The young man running the boat was not quite sure how to find my mooring. But the launch driver also monitors 68.

"I'll meet you at the end of the breakwater," he told the lad, "and lead you out to *MoonWind*."

And so, at quarter to seven, I got pumped out. So did the visiting team. I turned my radio off, checked my circuits, and secured my companionway. The launch driver hove to nearby then took me ashore.

"Didn't think you planned to sleep aboard," he said. "Another ten minutes and you'd have been stranded out here."

"Oh, no," I replied. "I'd have had the pump-out boat put me ashore. After six hours of making me wait, that was the least he'd have done."

I should have gone sailing instead. In six hours I could have sailed out far enough to pump my tank over the side. With such a good breeze, I might have had something worthwhile to write about.

Arrghhh!

Without the Cry of the Gull

I'm spending the night aboard *MoonWind* at her mooring. There's a lovely though not a spectacular sunset over Groton Long Point: a pale, streaky sky with smoky wisps that dissipate from our smoldering star now settled amid the trees.

Went out today but, as usual, started late and didn't clear West Cove till half past lunchtime. SailFlow predicted ten to fifteen knots, but it seldom exceeded half that. By the time I reached Latimer Ledge it was three o'clock. There's no safe place to anchor save Napatree between Latimer and Point Judith Pond, twenty miles away. Napatree lay merely two miles off. Arriving at Point Judith at midnight held no appeal. If the wind should fail in the afternoon, as it's wont to do this time of year, I might not even arrive in time for breakfast. At two knots, you mustn't plan to see too much of the world.

So I messed about off Stonington then beat my way home to Noank. The breeze picked up until I was making four knots, but at four o'clock died away to a mocking whisper. I felt fortunate to maintain a half knot against the tide. Off Whaleback Rock I discovered a little bundle of breeze that someone had tucked away in case of a lull. I tore off a piece and stuffed it into my sails, then wafted back to my nearby mooring with steerageway to spare.

Made some green tea and tuned in *Prairie Home Companion* and thought about some supper. I'd forgotten the olive oil. Although my pans are Teflon-coated, I heard a lot of grumbling from the onions: the usual rant about lack of consideration. Even being an onion has its drawbacks.

Now the absent sun under-lights the clouds with a pink profusion. The harbor ripples placidly about me; the fleet of sailing craft all duly face to watch the sun's departure. They gently sway to the nearly elusive music of the waters.

The sky due west ripples to red as the eastern horizon fades to various shades of slate and pewter. The dome high above retains the blue of a much-washed denim shirt. So quickly do the colors change, does the light devolve, does the texture of the firmament flex silently with an animus of its own.

As the night comes on, our local pyromaniacs ignite the last of their Independence Day arsenal. First, a few feckless displays reveal the beach; later, the pulse and rumble of heavy artillery shake the sky. This from the mouth of the Thames four miles distant.

By ten o'clock the harbor spreads dark and silent.

When I wake I lie in indolent reverie as Sunday morning dilates. The curtains are off the boat to be cleaned and repaired, and *Moon-Wind*'s snug white cabin diffuses the dawn. As the sun streams through the port lights I bestir myself with reproaches for wasting the day. It is six o'clock. I routinely stretch and exercise fifteen minutes, then put on the kettle. By half past six I've settled into the cockpit with my notebook and mug of coffee.

Today I shall ride the last hour of the ebb to the foot of Fishers Island; cut through Wicopesset Pass, tack most of the twelve miles out toward Montauk Point; tack the same distance to the Race and through it with the last of the flood; then run before the westerly wind back to West Cove again. A voyage of twenty-five miles or more with the helpful tide on my quarter. It certainly seems a plausible run for my little boat on this lovely summer's day.

Certainly, the tide is predictable—within approximate limits. By the time I finish my journal, make some breakfast, square away the cabin, and mend a batten pocket, I expect the breeze to wake and prove cooperative. For now a two-knot tempest troubles the tide that slowly escapes the harbor.

A single gull flaps the width of West Cove, lamenting. Had I but as short a life as hers my wings should never be still. Jib and mains'l must serve me as wings for now and, though my lament is decades long, it is liberally interspersed with jubilation. Surely the world awaits my glad involvement. How should I fail to share the creed of the wind? And how should I thrive without the cry of the gull, the sob of the sea?

Maybe Colder

When I arose at daybreak it was twenty-two degrees. I snuggled up to my mug of strong, dark French roast and clicked on the Weather Channel.

"Cold today," it admonished. "Maybe colder." By eight o'clock it had surged to twenty-four—the high for the day. I accountably grew affectionate toward the woodstove. My crew called up, as promised, at nine o'clock.

"Ready to sail?" she chortled.

I put on both my union suits, three pair of wool socks, two watch caps, and my mittens. I took my cell phone and started out the door.

"Don't you plan to finish dressing?" my observant wife inquired.

Eventually, I clambered into my truck. Then I practiced skidding about on that pond I call my driveway. Did I mention we had a sleet storm night before last? It began as snow but considerately converted into icing. Fortunately, I brought a box of birthday candles to decorate my boat.

As I'd thoughtfully left enough ice in my drive to propitiate the gods, I slid sideways into the road, executed a 720, and set a course for the boatyard.

I hadn't had time enough yesterday to spare a thought for *Moon-Wind.* This morning I found her liberally sheathed in ice. The tarpaulin I'd bought two months ago to drape her boom and keep her deckhouse and cockpit dry remained below in the vee berth, neatly folded. I leapt up on deck, executed a pretty slalom around the standing rigging, slid across the hatch on my starboard ear, and tumbled into the cockpit. The tiller went up one sleeve and came out the other.

I strapped on my crampons, grabbed my ax, and assaulted the wolves of winter. By the time my smiling crew appeared, I had freed the main hatch enough to remove the drop boards.

"Isn't it lovely today?" she said.

"Yes," I replied, heaving a chunk of crusty ice overboard. "When do we get our share of global warming?"

"But the sun is shining," she said. "And the clouds look fluffy as fleecy white lambs, and all of West Cove is filled with little ripples."

She peered beyond the breakwater. "Well, little whitecaps, anyway."

"Here are some lobsterman's rubber gloves and a mallet," I grumped. "Pipe down and break some ice."

After an hour we had the boat half clear. But the nonskid coating on the deck proved itself anything but. And the powdery ice left behind had as much traction as marbles. Any spray we shipped today would form a glaze on deck. Sliding about on a pitching boat would soon cease to amuse. Beneath the boom, the mainsheet hung in a massive, frozen coil. I hadn't a cooking pot large enough to poach the entire thing.

"We aren't going out," I informed my crew. "The chamber of commerce doesn't recommend swimming in December."

"How stodgy of them," she said.

We draped my tarpaulin over the boom, over the lifelines, and secured it to the bases of the stanchions with foot-long pendants. Tying knots in little pieces of line requires fingers. I worked without my gloves for a half hour. Of course, I needed to clear loose ice around each stanchion base. After I'd put the second half hitch in my little finger, I knew it was time for a break.

There weren't enough stanchion bases for all the grommets. I thawed out my best red pencil to revise my thinking. I found two lengths of seven-sixteenths braid in my cockpit locker. On either side, I secured an end to the base of a stanchion forward of the mast and streamed the line aft, threading it through both loops of each stanchion base. Then I belayed the end to a cleat on my coaming.

Now I had something continuous to which to fasten my pendants.

125

To avoid abrading the canvas, I padded the tops of my stanchions with strips of carpet, folded over and seized with rigging tape.

I now had a tent that came nearly to the deck. It was cozy inside: light and windless and, comparatively, warm. I managed to pull on my gloves with only my teeth.

We walked up the hill to Carson's. The midday sun was bright; the wind was cool; the flush of vigorous health adorned our cheeks. We hung our coats on the floor and sat at the counter. I straightened each finger tentatively until I could ease off my gloves. The waitress gave me a cheery smile.

"Isn't it lovely today?" she said. "The sun is shining and the clouds look fluffy as fleecy white lambs, and . . ."

"Pipe down, lass," I growled, "and pour the coffee."

The Universal, Noank, Connecticut

12 January

Yesterday was as glorious a day as any of us in New England has any right to expect: nearly fifty, partly sunny, an eight-knot breeze, and the waters of Fishers Island Sound a soft, rippled carpet of blue.

We backed *Moon Wind* out of her slip and motored out the channel. I gave the helm to my crew and raised our rags. Although the zephyr scarcely heeled *Moon Wind,* I chose to bend on my brand-new storm jib—just to get out the wrinkles. Nothing crinkles more than a fresh-sewn sail. Besides, the bronze hanks glistened and needed some tarnish.

It's embarrassing to have only *some* bronze hardware that glistens. It necessitates your polishing every piece of hardware on your boat. If you do that, then you need to varnish all your brightwork, then buff and wax your gel coat, then wash your running rigging. Once you start to clean a boat, there's no telling where it may take you. And the worst of it is, it takes time away from sailing.

Life's too short not to sail twenty-four hours a day. There's a fellow a few slips over from mine who spends his weekends cleaning and painting his sloop. He never goes out. He shudders when he sees me come in with sea salt on my grab rails. I watch him surreptitiously every summer. Twenty-three coats of varnish he puts on his coamings. He buffs his deckhouse every single weekend. He keeps his steering wheel so bright I can't endure to look at it.

I watched a seagull smash a crab and eviscerate it on his cabin top one day. It's been a while since I saw a sailor cry.

Now that it's winter, his boat is covered in canvas, tightly stretched over a wooden frame. Now, every artist knows exactly what a stretched canvas is for, and many of our gulls in West Cove studied under Jackson Pollock and at times feel urgent needs to express themselves.

I keep *my* self-expression under control. Whenever *I* feel urges, I go sailing.

Though the sun was half obscured about half the time, the afternoon proved bright and cheery although a tad bit chilly. The altostratus panoply was stretched and streaky and gray and white, and obscured the windward sky. As the moisture in the cloud cover crystallized, a sun dog's colorful muzzle poked through the clouds.

Aside from a small commercial fishing boat and a couple of skiffs commuting to Fishers Island, we had the sea to ourselves. Not a sail to be seen in any direction. Most sailors think of winter sailing as something for frostbite racers: little boats in some sheltered waters scooting from mark to mark. Why should that be? There must be close to a hundred boats that winter wet at West Cove. But many sailors have covered their boats. Many have removed their booms—taken them home to mount over their mantels to show to friends.

"Yes, that's the boom from *Sea Puss*. Quite the boat! I remember I took her out one afternoon back in July. Made it nearly all the way past the breakwater."

I don't pretend to be resistant to cold and ice and snow and wayward penguins. But on a fine day in winter, what can be more rewarding than to mess about on the sea for a little while? Of course you need winter clothing—this isn't the season to flaunt your naked self to the opposite sex. They'd be too cold to be responsive, anyhow. And our harbor seals think we look funny, with or without clothing.

"Pull your watch cap over your ears, pull your collar up to break the wind, quit your whingin', and take the helm while I pry that frozen merganser out of the cringle."

When you get too cold to feel your nose, come about on the other tack so the sun shines into the cockpit. Take along a thermos of something hot. Remember that you've winterized your head, so bring a bucket. Sunglasses are a must as the sun will be low in the sky, even at noon. And don't forget your boat hook. You'll need it to beat your crew when they start to complain about the cold. There's nothing like a good flogging to improve the circulation.

By four o'clock (sixteen hundred to all you *real* sailors) the sun has begun to think about retirement. It's best to head back to your slip before your nose bilge turns into icicles. And a hot log fire and a cup of steaming chocolate will help restore flexibility to your fingers.

Just don't overdo it. Self-indulgence makes us weak—prone to all the ailments known to man. Keep your house at fifty degrees and bathe in cold salt water. Leave some windows open all winter so you always know which way the wind is blowing. You *are* a sailor, aren't you? Central heating is very much overrated. So is hot running water. Real men and real women don't need all that sissified stuff in order to be content.

Just ask my wife.

Late Winter's Sail

They threatened fifty degrees this afternoon. Of course, they lied, but they got me excited enough to bend on my sails and back *Moon-Wind* out of her slip and go gallivanting down the sound to count the herring gulls. The reason I got so excited was I hadn't been out sailing since the first week of December. Imagine that! Me, the inveterate whatyoumaycallit, who goes out sailing whenever the mercury gets ecstatic from the all-too-meager attention of our sun at this time of year.

I buckled on my genuine secondhand wet suit and my rubber booties to match, in case the big bad ocean decided to souse me, and drove the seven miles down to the boatyard. In order to winter wet, I have to move *Moon Wind* back to this marina where I used to work and used to keep her year-round, before I got so high-tone that I joined a fancy yacht club. Thing is, our yacht club has the same sort of laid-back folks who populate the marina, so I now have a fresh population on whom to inflict my stories.

But the yacht club won't let me winter wet in my slip. Guess they're afraid I might go sailing after December the first and set a bad example for other members. Might start a fad or something. Like frostbite racing or ice boating or going out on lovely winter days when the air is over forty and the water isn't quite solid.

Not that the water gets solid much hereabouts anymore. The oldest geezer I've ever known told me only thirdhand that the estuary we know as the Thames River, which is deep enough to hide the submarines they build alongside it, used to freeze over. Not only that, but all of Fishers Island Sound, a couple of miles in width, used to freeze over. Word is, you could drive your brand-new Model T truck down the Thames River and right on across the sound to Fishers Island.

Nowadays, if we get an inch of ice in our slip, we rouse up and make a proclamation and ask what the world's coming to. Having recently—last week, as a matter of fact—been voted a provisional member of the Junior Geezers Club, I can now remember things accurately as far back as the '50s. In those days, the Connecticut River used to freeze across several inches thick, a couple of feet of brackish tide notwithstanding. But the little tankers that carried heating oil up river to Hartford ran every day and could usually keep the channel clear by themselves. Occasionally, we'd get a severe cold snap—subzero weather, by golly—and the Coast Guard would have to send an icebreaker up to clear the channel.

We had winter in them days, children. The Woolly Mammoth used to hang out by our woodstove to thaw his nose. But today it was balmy. Forty-three in New London, according to the voice on my VHF. Of course, I was under way before I heard this and *MoonWind* wouldn't return to her slip until she'd sailed the algae off her bottom. The thermometer in my kitchen window had said just over fifty, but it only wanted to get me outside to do some work in the garden. I fooled it and played with my boat instead. Imagine doing yard work while the sun shines and a lovely ten-knot breeze ruffles the sound.

Anyway, I counted all the herring gulls—maybe some of them twice—and wrote a report that I sent to the Bureau of Vital Seagull Statistics in Kennebunkport. Now I can declare my sail as a business trip and write off the twenty cents' worth of gas I expended to get *MoonWind* in and out of the harbor. My accountant assures me that, in the interests of solvency, I should sail my boat as often as I can. For once I have to agree with my accountant. If only I could find some way to earn the next twenty cents.

MYSTIC HARBOR

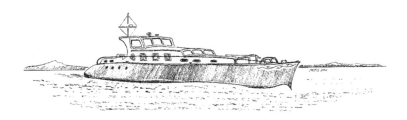

APHRODITE 1937

Wooden Boat Parade

Sunday I arrive at the boatyard about eleven. The flag droops on its pole; Fishers Island and the Dumplings are a muted gray-blue; the few sails on the sound drift unresponsively on the tide.

The launch driver has a large striped beach umbrella rigged above his console. We stand beneath it, chatting, as he motors me out to *MoonWind*. Our launch is an old Halsey Herreshoff that steers with a four-foot joy stick. It has a stout, brass banister for mounting its stair and a broad, brightwork rail.

"Good varnishin' weather," says the driver.

He knows I've spent the entire week varnishing the rails on a trawler.

"You come across a breeze in your travels, you tell it to come by here and pay me a visit," I suggest.

I take my tools aboard and go to work.

I remove the latch that keeps my outboard motor amidships, hammer it into a semblance of its once effective shape, and replace it. I remove the loose screw securing my port winch. How to keep it from backing out again? I take my Channel Locks and abuse the threads just a bit, then replace the screw. It is difficult to insert, which gives me hope. I replace the frayed downhaul. I scrub the cabin sole.

Having spent all day Saturday as well working aboard, I decide enough is enough; I need to go somewhere. *MoonWind* feels the same. She begins to champ at her mooring pendant. I hank on my 150 genoa, secure it with a bungee to the foredeck, and rig the jib sheets. The cove has scarcely a ripple, but my motor is in the water. I check my fuel and swap the pickup hose to the fuller tank.

The motor, bless its little pistons, fires right up and, after the choke disengages itself, makes contented motor sounds. I leave my mainsail covered. In case of a breeze, the genoa should suffice. I cast off, motor past the end of Mouse Island, and turn up the Mystic River. If nothing else, I can always admire larger moored boats and salivate a little. *MoonWind* doesn't approve of my wish to purchase a larger boat but, then again, she knows I don't have any money. She humors me.

Just upriver I come upon an acquaintance on her mooring, scrubbing her boat.

"Oh," she says. "Are you on your way up to Mystic to watch the parade?"

I have to confess this event has slipped my mind. Mystic Seaport hosts a water parade of wooden boats. It is due to start in an hour. I throttle down to an idle and ascend the mile and a half to the railroad trestle as slowly as possible. Alongside the channel, boats are anchored in anticipation; people eat and drink and swim, and keep their cameras ready.

When I reach the trestle, I slowly come about and head downstream. Upstream, a cannon booms. Both the bridges open; the parade commences. First comes the police skiff, blue light pulsing. Just astern, the Seaport steam excursion boat, *Sabino*, laden with sightseers, plows her way. Behind her come a couple of miles of beautiful wooden craft from a bygone era.

I keep to one side of the channel and let them pass me. I have the best seat in the house. The *Sabino* ensconces herself at a pier downriver and proceeds to broadcast a commentary on each boat in the procession. Firstly come powerboats of every description, from a little Penn Yan runabout to the seventy-four-foot *Aphrodite* from Watch Hill, with her mirror-like blue, whaleback hull and glistening acre of brightwork. Sailboats follow. On a lovely old sixty-foot sloop, an accordion, a fiddle, two penny whistles, and a tambourine play "Popeye the Sailor Man." A barefoot lady in an ankle-length dress dances languorously upon the fantail. In the eyes of a stately ketch, four kilted pipers and an athletic drummer perform a rousing air.

As I motor past *Sabino,* a little fiberglass catboat scoots out from among the piers on the Noank shore and cuts across my bows. The breeze has awoken enough to allow her plenty of steerageway. She clears me by several yards and enters the channel. The channel is slightly busy for a mile in either direction. The little boat tacks and comes directly at me. I shear off toward a heavily planked retaining wall that runs alongside the channel. The little boat crowds me closer and closer, forcing me to the wall. She's scarcely an arm's length away. The young man in her looks the opposite way.

"Do you think you could spare me a fathom, lad?" I shout.

"You're under power, so *I* have the right-of-way," he sneers. "Or don't you understand that?"

I slam my motor into reverse and he scoots beneath my bow. Yes, he has the right-of-way, but entering a busy channel and playing about in it, forcing yourself into harm's way, seems arrogant to me. He could have crossed to the mooring field, the other side of the channel, played among the moored boats there and watched the whole parade.

I wait for a gap in the procession, throttle up, and cross the channel. My acquaintance on her mooring clicks picture after picture.

"Aren't they splendid!" she says.

I continue along the edge of the mooring field. I sneak into the channel at the mouth of the harbor and follow a sixty-eight-foot schooner to where she makes her turn. The parade is over. I wend the channel past the stately lighthouse at Morgan Point, round Mouse Island, and head home to West Cove.

On my mooring, I square away *MoonWind,* then hail the launch on channel 68.

I'm so busy making up yarns about the parade to amaze the launch driver that I leave my cellular phone behind in my cockpit.

Hello, Hello, Hello!

March the twentieth marked the first day of spring. I didn't believe it. It was several degrees below the freezing mark first thing in the morning and the wind howled about my house at twenty knots, and gusted to nearly thirty. The clouds grew ugly and gray and extroverted. It didn't seem fair to those crocuses I'd uncovered with my rake the day before. I dashed outside and gave them all hot coffee with lots of sugar.

On Friday, the twenty-first, the lions of March roared and displayed their fangs. The lambs remained in hiding. Fishers Island Sound turned tall and frothy. Thirty- to forty-knot gusts set the standing rigging on *MoonWind* keening. Helios finally heard her mournful complaint. Urging his steeds, he drove his flaming chariot across the pale sky. The day grew bright, but the winds still had their way.

The twenty-second dawned fair and cold and calm. Perhaps *this* is spring, I thought. In the forenoon, I removed the cover from *Moon-Wind*. I hanked on a jib, started the motor, and backed her out of her slip. The breeze blew a mere ten knots; the sun regaled; the temperature soared to forty-seven degrees.

On my way to North Dumpling, I surprised a seal in search of a bit of lunch. With so many lobster pots to choose from, she shouldn't have a problem.

I sailed against the wind and tide for two hours and made about two miles. I finally tacked and headed toward Mumford Cove, but set and drift brought me quickly back toward Noank. Well, I thought, I'll slip into Mystic Harbor and chase some ducks. By pointing thirty degrees above the course I actually wanted I had a good chance of fetching the narrow entrance to the harbor.

The breeze grew suddenly fitful. It laid me over, then veered around to the north. It backed just a bit, and just in time, to allow me to clear the first marker. Inside the shelter of Morgan Point, it waned to a gentle breeze with occasional gusts. I beat my way through the mooring field and made my way back to the channel. If I pinched too much, the ebb tide shoved me about. The dogleg halfway up the harbor allowed me to let out my sails.

Aside from playing the wind, I had to admire the lack of boats in the water. Those few in slips were mostly covered over. This apathy for a lovely Saturday afternoon overwhelmed me. I watched a pair of mariners poke beneath the cover on their sloop.

"Yep, she's still in there, Maggie."

By Memorial Day, when they finally launch, they'll complain of the lack of wind.

Just ahead, the Amtrak Acela rattled loudly across the railroad trestle. A minute later, the breeze temporarily veered and began to stall me. I put the helm over quickly while I still had way, backed both main and jib, and spun her hard. I managed to stay within the narrow channel and rode the last of the ebb back toward the sound.

The wind blew mostly abeam now. As I passed the head of Mason Island, a hundred yards offshore, someone hailed me. A grizzled man, in a bright red shirt, waved energetically from his deck.

"Hello, hello, hello, hello!" he shouted.

I gave him an understanding wave from beneath my straining sail. I knew he wished he could come aboard to soak the breeze and sunlight into his system. Spring is a time of birth, of rejuvenation. If you leave your mirror, you needn't see all that gray hair. You need only ride the wind, embrace the sea.

I could nearly stay in the channel traversing the dogleg by Sixpenny Island. Fortunately, there was plenty of water in the mooring field downwind. I missed the last nun by twenty feet, turned and fell off the wind. I wafted by the nearly deserted piers of somnolent businesses: Ford's Lobsters, Haring's Marina, Abbott's Lobsters, Maxwell's Boatyard, Noank Shipyard. A half mile ahead of me spread the sound.

Suddenly I saw a sailing dinghy charging across the mile-wide mouth of the harbor. She headed for me at full tilt and might have cut me off but, just then, a skiff came up the harbor and intercepted her. The dinghy slewed abruptly into the wind. Her tight maneuver laid her over forty-five degrees. The skiff's skipper took the dinghy in tow. Grumpy father reprimands errant son, I guessed.

Ahead of me, the skiff towed the dinghy past Morgan Point, around Mouse Island, and halfway into West Cove, then released her. The dinghy promptly followed the skiff back out to the sound. As I dropped my sails by our mooring field, they rode side by side, a half mile away, loudly debating the wetness of the water.

I gentled *MoonWind* into her slip and made her all-a-taut-o. I couldn't have been blessed with a lovelier day. Assured that spring had finally arrived, I stopped by a drainage ditch on my drive back home and conducted a rousing chorus of eighty-four peep frogs.

Mystic Seaport

Yesterday I arrived at the club about ten o'clock and couldn't find my boat. Not that she wasn't there, waiting for me. I'd already told her we were going out for the day and had messed about with her rigging and replaced a couple of battens. I'd also replaced her fuel filter and one of the fuel line fittings and filled her tank with fresh gas.

But *MoonWind* was not to be seen.

"Where's my boat?" I inquired of the launch driver.

"Here," he said. "You grab this corner of the fog and I'll take this corner. Now, lift."

We picked up the near edge of the fog and peeked beneath it and, sure enough, there was little *MoonWind* on her mooring.

"How about we roll this up and stow it beneath the clubhouse for later?" I asked.

"I'm a bit shorthanded," he said. "Just wait awhile; it's sure to burn off before it's time for supper."

I figured that, while I waited, I might as well do something constructive. I persuaded the launch drive to motor me out to *MoonWind*. After a bit of judicious groping, I managed to find her toe rail and clambered aboard. I started the motor and, using my GPS, managed to motor the two hundred yards to the work slip and made fast. Then I got to play with the hose and the brush. *MoonWind* had, unaccountably, gotten rather dirty these past few weeks while I was off extravagating about the Virgin Islands.

First I thinned the radishes that were growing in the scuppers. Then I attacked the alfalfa sprouts that had taken refuge in the locker that holds the spare fuel tank. It's wonderfully easy to have a small produce garden aboard your boat. All you need is some guano, and maybe a few dozen earthworms to keep it aerated. Our local gulls prove more than cooperative when it comes to guano.

After I finished tending my garden I scrubbed my grubby vessel inside and out. I used so much water that I blew out the water main. The commodore of the club, himself, came down the pier to commend me. At least my boat was clean, for today I was entertaining a famous publisher: none other than Diane Buccheri, founder of *Ocean Magazine*. A quarterly, *Ocean* addresses all aspects of the sea, from ecological issues to search and rescue; from whale song to windsurfing; from poetry and stories of storms and sunsets, to stunning photographs of the surf as it ravishes the shore.

By the time she arrived, you could see as far as our breakwater without a telescope. This gave me hope that the fog might clear, as the breakwater is a quarter mile away. I squared away *MoonWind* and bent on my largest jib. This might prove helpful in case we encountered a breeze. Just now, I could see my reflection in the harbor. As this proved a rather alarming manifestation, I did my best to keep my eyes averted.

Eventually, we cast off under power and felt our way out of the harbor. Out in Fishers Island Sound, visibility had improved to about a mile. By early July, we consider this a clear day. We hoisted our sails and pretended the wind was blowing. By the time we reached Noank, four miles to the east, we made three knots.

My publisher kept her camera occupied. We met a grim, dark schooner emerging from the haze. She proved to be the *Amistad:* the replica of that sinister ship that transported slaves to our shores in the nineteenth century. We met the schooner *Argia* that takes sightseers from Mystic down to the sound.

We entered Mystic Harbor, wing and wing, and wended our way to the pier at Noank Shipyard. There we made fast for an hour to get some lunch. The elderly man on the fifty-foot cabin cruiser across the pier helped us tie up.

"You know what happens when you kiss a frog?" he asked my companion.

"Does he turn into a storyteller?" she asked. She wasn't in the market for a prince. As any editor will attest, storytellers are always in more demand than princes, as they're willing to write for much less pay per word.

"Come aboard and see my frog," said the skipper.

We dutifully went aboard. Seated in a chair in the main salon was a six-foot-high bronze frog with a bronze can of beer. A sculptor in South Carolina had created him. The skipper had purchased his frog en route from the islands. I only hope the resultant prince will be a little more limber.

We continued to Costello's: our local clam shack. There we each had a delicious lobster roll. We sat on the upper deck and watched a seagull on the pier below dismember an unwilling crab, but we had the advantage—we got coleslaw and chips with our crustacean. We talked of possums, of kittens, and of the sea; of North Carolina's Outer Banks; of windsurfing and muskrats. We returned to our boat and applied a bit more sunblock. The haze had totally burned away and, although we heard distant rumbling from a thunderhead downwind, we enjoyed as lovely a day as we deserved.

We motored up the harbor to the village. There we found the railroad swing bridge open. We passed through, then idled about the bascule bridge until its scheduled opening ten minutes later. My publisher took picture of the bridges, the village, the river, the beautiful boats. She wore a quarter inch off her shutter finger. We passed by the tall ship *Mystic,* tied at her charter pier. We sailed by Mystic Seaport in the hope that some of the beautiful wooden vessels from the previous weekend's show would still be there, but all had departed.

We came about and made our way back to the bascule bridge. We had hoped to sail down the harbor, but the wind had shifted and again blew from dead ahead. As the bridge opened, we saw, downstream, the *Amistad* and, behind her, the smaller *Argia* ascend the river. Once downstream, we looked back. As the two schooners passed beside the upraised deck of the bascule bridge, they, and the tall ship *Mystic* just upstream, were juxtaposed in an interesting composition of masts and rigging.

At the mouth of the harbor, I turned to the east behind Ram Island to head for St. Edmund's Retreat with its massive seawall. In 1954, Alys Enders willed her estate to the order of St. Edmund. As the need for a novitiate diminished, the Catholic Church determined to use the eleven-acre island as a retreat, both for spiritual leaders and for those undergoing rehabilitation. St. Edmund's has proved both a bulwark against the sea and a bastion of spirituality.

We came up into the wind and hoisted our sails. The breeze had picked up to eight or ten knots and we made good time with the flood tide returning to Pine Island. Just off Groton Long Point, we encountered the regatta of Wednesday-night racers. This melee of dozens of sloops, most of them larger than *MoonWind,* stretched the entire width of the sound. I managed to wend among a half dozen boats flying their spinnakers without discommoding any. Being on course for the final leg of the race, I came in fourth.

We arrived at Shennecossett too late for launch service. At Pine Island bell, I dropped my mainsail into the lazy jacks, and wafted to the pier using only my genny. I dropped off my publisher, wished her well, took my yellow kayak out of my truck, loaded it aboard, motored *MoonWind* back to her mooring, squared her away, and paddled back to the pier in time for twilight.

I noticed that the launch driver had taken my advice: Beneath the clubhouse I saw a huge roll comprising that morning's fog.

FISHERS ISLAND SOUND

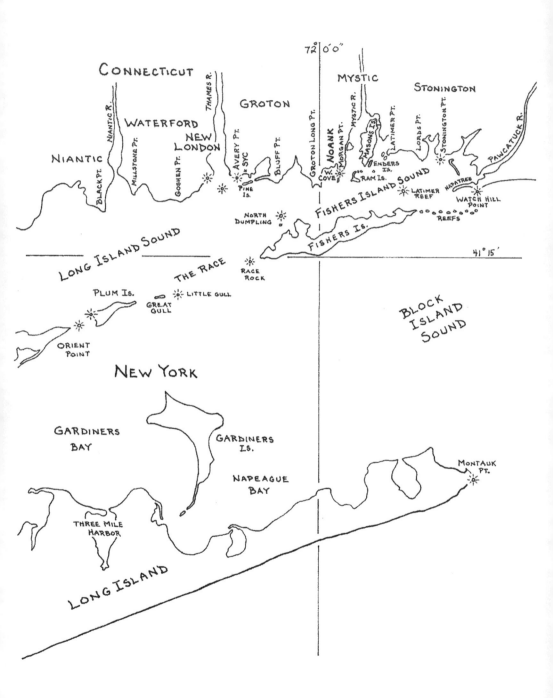

As a Kitten, As Well

This weekend we headed for the Connecticut River via Long Island Sound. We motored out of Noank to find the wind blowing out of the west—the way we presumed to head. We motored nearly to North Dumpling, hauled up our rags, and continued toward Race Rock. The breeze blew a steady ten knots; the tide ebbed against us.

Tomorrow, I thought, this same tide and wind can bring me back from Old Saybrook quick like a bunny. Today, the bunny would have to tack a few times. We wended the lobster pot buoys north of the Race and came within a half mile of the Rock. Race Rock, off the west end of Fishers Island, has a lighthouse on it. Between the Rock and Race Point on the island runs a navigable passage quarter mile in width. To the west stretches the Race: a playground five miles across between Race Rock and Plum Island off Orient Point. Here the Atlantic exchanges a million acres of tide with most of Long Island Sound. The reef beneath the Race produces fierce currents and heavy chop.

I sailed out here in my little Cape Dory Typhoon one time and attempted to round Race Rock from the west. Besides encountering chop, I met a four-knot rip that prevented me. While I strove against the tide, I saw a larger boat, perhaps a thirty-five-foot sloop, blithely riding the incoming rip between the Rock and Race Point.

She found herself set westward—careering toward Race Rock with scant control. I saw her stick pass behind the lighthouse and waited to hear the crash. She couldn't have missed being smashed on the Rock by more than half her length.

It amazes me that mariners don't consult their charts, or Eldridge's, or the common sense that the fairies leave under our pillows. Bucking the rip, I had only to jibe or come about to be swept away from danger. The Race is not a playground for the ignorant.

This afternoon, we tacked and headed northwest—away from the Race. The tide and wind together still thwarted our progress. By the time we reached the mouth of the Thames, five miles from Noank, three hours had expired; we wouldn't make the Connecticut in time to have dessert. I dropped the sails and started my outboard motor.

We made it as far as Bartlett's Reef, another couple of miles upwind, when the motor suddenly died. It started again but died within a few minutes. The afternoon wore on. We came about, hauled up only our genoa, and gently flew toward morning.

Behind Pine Island at the east shore of Thames's mouth lies a sheltered basin. We have friends who keep a boat there. They happen to be related to us but we forgive them that. We called them on our cellular phone and inquired about a berth. Of course, they said. We'll ask our harbormaster and call you back. Use the VHF, I suggested. All right, they said: Use channel 88.

In ten minutes we had our answer: A slip was available for the night, just a few down from theirs. They would come out in their dinghy and guide us in, and help us back into the slip. Fine, I answered. You ought to see me in a half hour, flying only my genny.

In a moment they called our cell phone. They hadn't heard my reply.

They met us at the harbor mouth. The breeze had abated and wafted us to the slip at less than a knot. Then we luffed and doused our rags, and warped stern-first between the pairs of pilings. Easy as pie. But you don't get pie until you finish your supper. As usual, we arrived just in time to eat.

It bothered me that they hadn't heard my response on the VHF. They stood on the pier with their handheld; I stayed aboard. We went through every channel on my set. Several others gave the same result: I could receive but not transmit. I carefully made a list of all those stations that worked both ways.

How about you, I queried: Can you transmit on every station on which you receive a signal? They hadn't thought about it. We dutifully progressed from station to station with similar results. It gratified me to learn that I had no problem being heard on all the important channels such as 68 and 13. It's good to know that one can be heard by harbormasters and bridge tenders. Anchoring in the bait shop or sticking your mast through the railroad trestle is generally frowned upon.

We squared away our boat and went out to dinner.

The following morning, I put fresh gas in my second tank, dumped the old fuel from my water-separator cartridge, purged the carburetor, and hand-cranked the motor two or three thousand times. Eventually, it caught. I stopped and started it several times. It fired up each time and purred like a kitten: a cougar kitten—one with an attitude. After all, two-stroke motors tend to growl a bit. This one dates from the Reagan administration, and I recollect lots of growling from that era.

A four-stroke outboard would truly purr like a kitten. *As* a kitten, as well. The small, domestic variety. Fact is, our younger Pusslet sounds like an ancient two-stroke that needs new valves, while our older Pusslet's purrs are quite subdued. A quieter motor would be a delight, but our older Pusslet sheds a lot and often disciplines furniture with her claws. I'm not so sure those are attributes desirable in a motor. Having an outboard that clawed up the couch would infuriate my wife.

Boating; or, Growing Older

Finally took *MoonWind* out for a sail yesterday after having been shorebound for over a month. Seems as though winter means to pass us by. After the ice and snow and freezing rain that normally depress us, it makes for a welcome change. I understand that the alligators have taken over the Chesapeake and the coconut palms grown so prolific that the entire eastern shore has been declared a hard hat area.

Yesterday, the breeze would scarcely lift your skirts, but the ebb tide ripped down Fishers Island Sound, determined to get to Watch Hill to see the moon rise. Since most fair-weather sailors tucked their boats in for the winter, the lobstermen have strung innumerable pots three ways to Sunday about the harbors. The ferocious tide drove some of these pot buoys well beneath the surface. We kept score and found that we nearly missed nearly as many buoys as we nearly hit.

With the wind and tide both out of the west, at every tack across the sound the tide set us back to about where we began. For those of you who stick close to your yards and crave a drier analogy, imagine riding your mower over and back just to mow the same swath again and again. Had we headed east with the wind astern, we could have made it to Boston in time for breakfast. If you find your grass has grown back as soon as you've mowed it, just turn your mower and drive due east. I'll meet you in Buzzards Bay.

Stopped at Mouse Island and interviewed the Old Cormorant, as promised. He couldn't remember a winter as mild as this one. He claimed the warmth of the water has led to proliferation of zooplankton, and consequently . . . My listening unaccountably grew impaired. I wonder if it's imperative that old folks bore us silly with their constant blather. I've asked lots of the younger generation about this phenomenon at great length, but usually receive only glazed stares in response.

So I've made it my resolution, this new year, not to grow any older. Some people say I won't be able to keep this resolution. Others confide I've done a remarkable job these past fifty years.

I say it's merely a matter of resolve. Given the choice of boating or growing older, I've made the only plausible decision. If my beard should happen to turn white, it'll be the result of not combing out salt spray.

After we bounced off two or three dozen lobster pot buoys, we made it out to West Clump. The tide was half out and, on the wet, exposed rocks, the seals basked in the sunshine. These seals enjoy vacation from Down East, where just staying warm this time of year counts as a full time job.

Following the holidays, they normally depart the coast of Maine for some well-deserved relaxation in tropical waters. Connecticut, with its sultry winters, pellucid depths, and sparkling sands, proves all the travel brochures can claim and, on days such as these, a bargain at half the price.

At least these seals know enough to keep off the piers and refrain from molesting our boats. Their cousins out west, the sea lions, seem to have no couth when it comes to boating. I've seen the photos. Dozens of portly pinnipeds, draped across pleasure boats in abandoned poses, sipping strong drink from glasses with tiny umbrellas. But everyone knows what Californians are like.

Our seals from Maine show much more reserve. You've only to converse with a lobsterman from Down East to know where they get their respect for well-built boats. And their reticent manners. Harbor seals seldom speak unless spoken to first, and then they usually just nod and say, "Ayuh."

January Sail

Yesterday it struggled to fifty degrees—the usual mix of sun and clouds with a few raucous seagulls thrown in to keep the mix lively. We put on our long johns, clipped our cell phones to them, and drove down to the boatyard.

Our poor old boat shop in Noank is gradually being dismantled. The shed on the north side has been removed, and the heavy electrical conduits that ran both through and beneath it have been separated from the wreckage. These will be rerouted to the nearest building.

For now, these cables ramp up out of a shallow, clawed-out depression, half filled with litter and broken glass and shingles. The clapboards where the shed was attached have mostly come away, leaving a half-open wall the length of the building, displaying hanging bits of board and bedraggled insulation.

We parked across the way from our ruinous shop. The double doors have been pried from the front, and we could look in at all the pathetic trash about the floor, and see, through the broken back windows, the piers and pilings and winter water beyond. The privacy of our old shop has been violated: a bereft old woman holding her skirts to her face to hide her anguish, exposing instead what no one would willingly see.

We averted our gaze and sidled to the next pier where *Moon Wind* lay patiently in her slip. As always, she greeted us gladly, eager to venture out, if only within the confines of Fishers Island Sound. I backed her out of the slip, turned, and motored into the channel. There was no one about. The boats at the piers were unpeopled; the moorings vacant.

But, out in the sound, three other sloops, two small commercial fishermen, and a solitary lobsterman took advantage of the mild afternoon. The wind blew gently, the tide ran out, the cool sun glimmered amid a straggle of clouds. I set a course for Flat Hammock, along the eastern edge of the shimmer, and crossed the placid sound.

Every so often, I had to swerve for a straining lobster pot buoy. The lobsterman, just ahead of me, tended his traps; circle, stop, pull up a trap, remove a few outraged lobsters, renew the bait, slide the trap over the rail.

This time of year, there are pot buoys everywhere. They nearly encroach on the channels. I presume my skeg and rudder will deflect the warps, though one time they did not. This isn't a good time of year to go over the side to disengage a pot warp from your rudder.

We entered West Harbor at Fishers Island and went as far as Goose Island. Between this sandy islet and the shore is a tenuous channel, indifferently marked. You need to know just where to zag—or was it zig? As the tide was rapidly running out, I came about without attempting the passage.

We slowly traipsed out of West Harbor. The outermost marks lie a quarter mile apart. I headed for the green can. South of this squats West Clump: a clutch of rocks just covered at high water. Yesterday, with the tide half out, they were nearly all exposed and draped with seals.

I rounded the can and we drifted by the rocks. The seals proved both curious and prudent. After they slipped or rolled into the water, they stuck up their sleek, wet heads and watched us intently. I, also, proved both curious and prudent. I kept several yards away from the rocks; I've been aground on West Clump and was not amused. One of the seals swam halfway out to *MoonWind* and poked up her head, but we hadn't any treats with which to reward her. We turned and wafted across to our marina.

The lobsterman continued to pull his pots. The two fishing boats lay together, end for end, sharing some coffee and taking a needful break from hauling nets. We entered the channel, passed Mouse Island, and whispered by the breakwater. The inner harbor scarcely divulged a ripple. One of the sloops, secure in her slip, was getting squared away; the other two followed us in. I put the motor into neutral and coasted into our slip.

The seals languidly held West Clump in place. The reclining breeze suspired. The ebb tide gradually slackened, and the sea resolved into slate and silver dimples. The lighthouse on North Dumpling posed: a statuesque silhouette. The molten sun spilled slowly into the sea.

LITTLE GULL LIGHT

THE RACE NEW YORK

Warm Enough to Sail

At daybreak, it was nearly forty. At noon, it was pushing fifty. I met my crew at the boatyard and we put *MoonWind* to rights. We had on our long johns and brought along coats and gloves. The water temperature was just a bit above freezing. The skin of ice on the Mystic River as I drove down the river road to Noank was just enough to support a few strutting gulls.

A fellow sailor on the pier was busily checking his boat and those of his friends.

"Lovely day," I said.

"Yes," he replied. "In only another month it'll be warm enough to sail."

"Think of that," I said.

We hanked on the smaller of my genoa jibs. It was blowing about twelve knots, but one never knows what treats await farther out. The tide would be high about two o'clock, and the wind blew from the northwest. It made most sense to head toward the Race—normally a turbulent spot but at slack water nothing to worry about. We would have both the wind and tide to bring us home.

We motored out of the harbor and hoisted our sails beyond the mooring field—destitute of boats this month of the year. I handed the helm to my eager crew and he set a course for Little Gull Light, about nine miles away.

The sailing was grand. We laid her over twenty degrees and rode the remaining tide for nearly two hours. We plowed through the Race—a little lumpy in places, but not rough enough for us to don our foul-weather gear. The lighthouse at Little Gull Island is a cylindrical, granite tower eighty-one feet in height with a jaunty red cap. Its light shines ninety-one feet above the water. Its dolorous horn re-

155

peats until you fear it will raise the dead. If it had they would have asked to borrow our mittens.

Frankly, I was more concerned about being in the shade of the mainsail. By this time, I had the helm. The sun was bright—I shouldn't have to shiver. I fell off a point to the south and the avid sun came pouring into the cockpit. Life was perfect.

Little Gull Island is so small that, at a mile distant, you could fit the whole thing in your pocket. Of course the aerial on the roof would probably get caught in your trousers when you tried to take it out to return it to some impatient Coast Guardsman.

Great Gull Island, just beyond, is a half mile in length. It's a sanctuary for birds, and covered with observation stations and nesting towers. It has a pier on the north side and a couple of minuscule cottages, one of which was slipping into the sea. It seems the Race is intent upon removing tons of soil and stone from various parts of the island. Perhaps this is the same soil that our marina paid so much to have removed last year from our slips and channel. I trust the dredging barge made the twenty-mile round trip to return it whence it came.

By the time we passed Great Gull it was time to come about and head for home. Florida would have to wait—at least until next weekend. The tide had turned; the wind was twelve to fourteen knots, occasionally gusting to twenty. What could be better? We tore through the Race, kindly avoided knocking over the Fishers Island Ferry leaving New London, and flew to West Cove with the fierce sun baking our backs. Aside from a couple of fishing boats, we hadn't seen a soul.

"Bet you're the first one out of West Cove this season," said my crew.

"Don't count on it," I replied.

Besides, each of us sailed our boat on the eighth of January. And two other sails were out in the sound that day. Being first, or last, or somewhere between, has never been my goal. My goal is to sail whenever the spirit moves me. If the wind is willing to move my boat as well, so much the better.

I'm not a frostbite racer. Those are the folks who determine your standing by counting all the icicles in your beard. This number is then multiplied by the waterline of your boat, divided by the windchill factor, and subtracted from the number of days since Christmas. This is commonly known as your handicap. Anyone whose handicap is warmer than minus twenty-four, Fahrenheit, is expected to buy the hot toddies after the race.

The entire purpose of frostbite racing appears to be stimulation.

A Flake of Green Paint

It was just below freezing at daybreak the last day of March, but it swiftly rose to fifty. By noontime, when I met my crew at the pier, it was as balmy as you should expect this time of year.

I parked my truck by the pier head, nearly beneath a sailboat who was having her bottom painted. A woman brandishing a roller was directing two young fellows she'd enlisted to help her. I asked her if my truck would be in her way. She didn't think so, but . . . I told her I would leave the keys in it. We began to discuss bottom paint and I proffered the advice to add plenty of extra paint where it would soonest wear away: the waterline and lead edges of the bow, keel and skeg. She thanked me for the advice and went straight to work. She could hear the enticement of the breeze upon the water; there wasn't a moment to lose.

I squared away *Moon Wind:* ran her motor, bent on a jib, uncovered my main, stowed my drop boards. We cast off and backed out of the slip. The wind, predicted to be from the northwest, was just a point east of south. The tide was on the ebb. Having to return by four o'clock, we headed west, against the tide; we would have it to bring us home.

Aside from the ferries to Orient Point, we saw but a handful of boats all afternoon. The first was another sailboat, which cleared West Cove a minute after we had. Another was a speedboat that overtook us later in the day. The UConn oceanographic vessel steamed forth from Avery Point and made her way easterly.

The sea stayed calm; the breeze blew about ten knots; the sun shone down with total regard for our comfort. These prove delightful days as long as you wear sufficient clothing. Watch caps and gloves are a must. We had but three or four hours to amuse ourselves. The wind veered a couple of points but kept us on a close reach going and coming. We couldn't find a thing to complain about and, consequently, had a miserable time.

However, we knew it would end too soon, and that made up for all the perfection we forced ourselves to endure.

Back in the shelter of West Cove at half past three, we found but half a breeze. We dropped the main and wrinkled up the channel with only our genny. I tilted the outboard into the drink and pushed the little black button. Touché! The motor responded by growling and spitting, but soon began to purr. I left it in neutral as we wafted toward our slip. I gave the helm to my crew and went forward. We made the first turn at two knots; I took the Genny across, but should have doused it.

I let the sheets go—about thirty yards too late. We lumbered into the slip a bit too quickly. My crew at the helm realized he didn't know how to shift my outboard motor into reverse. I snagged a cleat on the pier with the boat hook and found myself half off the boat, hanging on to the boom vang by my toes.

Eventually, I discovered myself on the pier. After I took a round turn on my ankle with the spring line, for security, I grabbed at a lifeline stanchion and was dragged the last five yards. We bumped the walkway pier ahead and removed a flake of green paint from *Moon-Wind's* prow.

Now we had something tangible to bitch about and felt the better for it. Were everything to go perfectly, what should I write about?

Out and Back

By the time you read this, I'll be back on the water. Though the weld on my gooseneck slide failed in a ferocious ten-knot April breeze, the welder did an admirable job and my rigging is all-a-taut-o. Before I went to the welder, I surfed the inevitable Internet for a new slide. In twenty minutes, I'd found one nearly identical to the 1970 artifact from my boat. One thing puzzled me, though. I never realized stainless steel cost five hundred dollars per pound. Nearly as much as lobsters during tourist season.

Went out yesterday afternoon to assure myself that the water was wet and the breeze as insistent as ever. Amazingly, I was not disappointed, again. Rode the tide on a close reach toward Watch Hill, where I determined to return along the outboard, southern, shore of Fishers Island. The first passage through the reef beyond the island I didn't consider, as I would need to head upwind. The second passage I all but passed, then came about and buried her nose in the breeze. I pinched her for all she was worth (the boat, dear, the boat), but fought a losing battle against the tide.

Fortunately, the passage was a hundred yards in width. I clawed my way between the two markers for fifteen minutes and made a quarter mile, but knew I wouldn't clear the rocks beyond. If I tacked I would set myself onto the reef. I tucked my tail between my legs, jibed her as tightly as I could, and was out of there in a twinkle.

I continued along the inside of the reef till I reached the lighthouse at Watch Hill Point that marks the open water. I hardened up and headed out to sea a mile, then tacked and tried again to stem the tide. Lessons in futility are abundant when you sail. The math is always apparent. Making three knots against a two-knot tide with twelve miles to go means that you won't be home for supper till they set the table for breakfast. Going the long way 'round about Fishers Island would add about five miles to my return.

I chose an ample passage back through the reef, and fell off the wind. The breeze picked up a trifle and I breasted the ebb a bit quicker than expected. By the time I was halfway back to Noank, the tide was in its final hour and scarcely slowed my progress. *Moon Wind* settled at fifteen degrees and nearly five knots and I made it back to West Cove on a single tack. I lifted my collar against the wind and contemplated hot tea.

A couple of miles from West Cove I overtook a thirty-foot sloop that berths three slips from *Moon Wind*. The end of last summer, she blew out her only jib. Or perhaps the north wind did it. The nuances of our language can be daunting. There are times when even my wife can scarcely understand me. Anyway, she (the sloop) was heading in with only her main and still making pretty fair time. When she gets her new genny, all I'll ever see of her will be her spreading wake.

Out and back and then at the pier, her skipper was learning the ropes to an avid lady. It's never too late to learn. There are still many things about boats I find confusing. Sometimes I get the Cunningham slightly confused with the catnip, and the Pusslet needs to loosen the luff instead of lying at home on the hearth with all four paws in the air.

We all of us have some lessons to learn, and with scarcely a century's span to learn them, it's a wonder we don't go aground much more than we do. The number of years I sat on sandbars, awaiting some extraordinary tide to raise me above myself, has set me back. The number of years I spent adrift could be a book by itself. And all those years I tacked up narrow channels against the current would make you weep.

The confident and careful mariner, mind and eyes wide open, usually makes a fair passage, and generally finds a snug harbor at its end. Just remember: never anchor out of your depth and you'll never reach the bitter end of your roding.

Rounding Fishers Island

Yesterday was as fair and as pleasant and as moderate as makes no difference, yet I encountered but a dozen sails at most upon the water in six hours. What is it people are waiting for? Not sun, nor warmth, nor a moderate breeze apparently. Here we are in the middle of May—the magnolias blown, the dogwoods filled, the maples unfurled—yet many boats hunker down on the hard, rock sullenly in their slips.

I actually planned my outing yesterday. I looked up the tide online before I started, not having purchased a current Eldridge's, and found that I could ride the ebb for two hours, then have the flood to aid me all afternoon. Then I went to SailFlow.com and checked the wind. Though much more problematic than the tide, I was assured that the wind—at that particular moment—was mainly from the north. When the wind is out of the north, you get to reach both ways along our local shore. From New York to Cape Cod, you can steer either 090 or 270 and never hit anything larger than an island. Believe me, many have tried.

Now that *MoonWind* resides in the mooring field, a bit of acrobatics is involved in the boarding process. I am finding more incentive to restore my Whitehall and get her into the water. Far more than to cut the lawn or prune the bushes. Climbing from my kayak into *MoonWind,* though it might improve my balance, certainly had little appeal when the ocean hovered at forty-five degrees. Merely the thought of freezing to death a hundred yards from shore encouraged me to maintain my equilibrium.

I tucked the kayak between the shrouds and the cabin trunk and secured her fore and aft. I started my motor but left it in neutral. I hoisted my jib and cast off the mooring pendant. The wind and tide carried me out of the harbor, where I raised my main and headed east toward Watch Hill.

What a perfect day to reach up the south shore of Fishers Island and take the long way home. The long way home seems preferable to most sailors, but I wouldn't dare to elaborate for fear of the wrath of the Lares and Penates. Not to mention a certain spouse who planned an evening meal.

At the end of Fishers Island, there extend a mile and a half of reefs with various passages through them. With this steady, eight-knot breeze, thought I . . . and just then, that breeze turned whimsical and veered and backed adeptly as a ballerina on tiptoes. Suddenly I had no breeze at all, blowing from out of the east, the southeast, the north, the northeast, the west. After twenty minutes of such pirouetting, it settled into nearly due south and my wind indicator stop rehearsing to become an anemometer.

I tacked though the reef and followed one tack for eight miles along the backside of Fishers. The breeze scarcely varied the rest of the afternoon. Must have been the changing tide or maybe a disagreement between Aeolus and Poseidon. I consulted my chart, punched in Race Rock on my GPS in case of a blinding snow squall, and had some lunch.

Admiring the cottages, which average twenty rooms, on the south shore of Fishers Island kept me amused for a couple of hours. I scanned the shore with binoculars and counted the panes of glass that winked in the sun. As I drew near the western, Race end of the island, I inspected the bunker left over from World War II, and watched little planes as they hurtled onto the airstrip by the shore. About this time, I was overtaken by an Ultimate 24, a high-tech racing boat. She disposed of me so swiftly that I carefully checked both my anchors to be sure they were still aboard.

I passed between Race Rock and the point and let my sails out. The four miles home I would run before the wind. The tide had taken me through the Race but would thwart me closer to home. I passed between the Dumplings and headed for Morgan Point. It was now five o'clock and the breeze was coming and going—mostly going. I dropped my main a half mile from my mooring and tried to sail in with just my jib. It appeared if I persisted in this procedure, I could very well be a trifle late for breakfast. I resigned myself to motoring to my mooring.

After I stowed my sails and squared away, I got to do my balancing act with my little yellow kayak, cheered by the raucous laughter of the gulls. The tide sped me gleefully back to the piers—to the world of work and worry.

Memorial Day 2007

Memorial Day weekend and warm and clear and *Moon Wind* gnawing at her halter, wanting to be set free of her mooring to splash in the pool. I still hadn't finished repairing the Whitehall, so we resorted to launch service—first time this season. What a delight to pile all of our gear aboard and step down into a large, stable boat with a sturdy brass banister to grasp. And, after being entertained by her venerable skipper, we hove alongside *Moon Wind* and had merely to step up six inches to get aboard.

No heaving dinghy that rocks precariously as you stand up; no errant dinghy that scoots from beneath your feet as you clamber aboard; no rocking-horse dinghy that tries to pitch you headfirst into the harbor. No lovely Whitehall pulling boat to follow you over the ocean and take you ashore. Had we all our choices, what would this world be like?

Our first choice of destination had been Pine Island, behind which our friends keep their Egg Harbor 33. When we called to pass on our intentions, they told us they were headed for Napatree—that sheltered anchorage behind Watch Hill. We decided to meet them there, raft together, and spend the night.

The tide was against us and the breeze was light, so it took two hours to make the handful of miles. But sailing is nowise all rail-down excitement. Traipsing along at two or three knots and admiring the sunshine keeps us occupied. Being as simple as we are, we've learned to be amused by simple things.

A bountiful haze enveloped the horizon and kept our visibility to five miles, but Impressionism needs distance for true appreciation. To have that lush blue haze come aboard would gain it no admiration.

Off Stonington, we ran before a reticent breeze that took liberties with our wind vane. Our genoa went from starboard to port and back again so often, I was forced to sail according to the wind. I managed to pass the mouth of Stonington harbor with a grumbling trawler bearing down, her booms awry, and speedboats bouncing about me. The entrance to the channel to Watch Hill is thirty yards wide: enough to accommodate numerous boats as long as one of them needn't tack too often. As we rounded Sandy Point, the breeze behaved. The genoa gladly filled to leeward and kept her shape the mile and a half to the mouth of the Pawcatuck River. There, we hardened up and reached the last half mile to Watch Hill.

Turned out our friends already had rafted with two other power cruisers. But their boat was on the outside, and downwind. I doused the jib and tiptoed up with the slacked main just adraw. I luffed her a bit too early, and we glided to a standstill three yards off. Our friends stood by with lines and fenders ready. I tossed the bowline to the grinning mate and, in moments, she secured us.

A pleasant evening ensued. We took our supper aboard the Egg Harbor and gossiped and ate and relaxed. We also refitted and repaired our boats with many declarative sentences. The children played and rowed a dinghy about and craved attention. Eventually, they were taken ashore to ride the carousel and smother in ice cream. The two of us stayed aboard as anchor watch. The yellow sun fell into the sea; the fifty boats swung about with the changing tide; the last of the terns was reabsorbed by the sand dunes; the gulls took a much-deserved rest upon the shoals.

It's been a while since I spent a night without setting an anchor. The four boats rode securely on two hooks. The night remained calm. As always, when I woke to inspect the plumbing, I dutifully checked on the anchor I hadn't set. The other skippers proved vigilant as well.

Sunday, we rose at seven and poured strong coffee over our heads. The little breeze hastened out of the northeast—nearly opposed to the breeze of the day before. *MoonWind* implored us to let her go play with the swans. We cast off and tucked our fenders into their locker.

Again we ran before the wind all the way back to Noank. I rigged my boom vang as a preventer by securing it to the base of a forward stanchion on the lee rail. When I first bought *MoonWind* I wondered why they'd provided three extra yards of line with the boom vang tackle.

The crew dozed on a cockpit cushion as I twiddled the tiller to keep the genoa filled. The sky slowly closed, but no way threatened. The haze had vanished. The mild waters lifted us up and agreed to hinder us home, but we managed three knots against the flowing tide. By eleven o'clock, I put the helm down and let go both the sheets. *MoonWind* approached and gently kissed her mooring buoy good morning.

Watch Hill, Rhode Island

An Uneventful Sail

Yesterday I had eight to ten knots all afternoon and a lovely, if totally uneventful, sail. I covered a bit more than twenty miles in a bit less than six hours. I never heeled much more than twenty degrees. The only time I hit five knots was returning through Wicopesset Pass with the surging tide behind me.

If something untoward doesn't happen to me soon, I may have to spin you a yarn.

People don't believe me when I tell them about my mermaid. They scowl when I try to explain to them the best way to scrub the barnacles from your bottom during a gale. From the bottom of your boat, that is. They roll their eyes at the tale of the sixty-pound lobster that chased me from Halifax to Port of Spain.

What's a storyteller to do? Stick to the unvarnished truth? Where I come from, everyone expects plenty of varnish—six to eight coats every spring. The little badger in our boat shop can scarcely keep up with our demand for brushes.

It's time I sanded down the brightwork on *Moon Wind*. It's beginning to yellow in places and I dread having to wood her again this year. But doing maintenance on a mooring has many drawbacks. Firstly, it's a long swim ashore if you find you've forgotten something. Such as your spouse. And secondly, the boat tends to bounce just when you're holding the varnish brush an inch from your partner's ear.

Removing varnish from your loved one's hair with a dull pair of scissors on a rocking boat seldom conduces to a pleasurable life afloat. Nor does pouring mineral spirits over her head and scrubbing vigorously with a Scotch-Brite pad. When all else fails, point your finger at the badger who made the brush. As usual, he's sitting on his ditty box, eating a cookie, and causing no trouble at all. But behaving myself has always proved the surest way to get myself into trouble. Why should the badger be exempt from the wrath of a glistening spouse?

When I fetched Wicopesset Pass on my outboard passage, the tide was pouring through it and the wind was dead abeam from Fishers Island. Both attempted to set me on the shoals on the eastern side. I headed as close to the island as I could and was swept to the center of the passage halfway through. I barely escaped the shoals—I should have headed fifty yards farther upwind and upcurrent before I entered the pass.

Tacking mid-passage is risky, and there comes a point when you're too close to the rocks to effect maneuvers. Losing steerageway for even seconds may spell ruin. You promise never to take Poseidon's name in vain—except during dire emergencies—and point as high as possible. I'm sure I missed those shoals by a good five yards.

And that was all the excitement I had the entire afternoon. The rest of the time I only enjoyed the sailing. I bucked the outgoing tide as I beat toward Montauk Point for half the afternoon, lost ground in the process, and headed back the way I came when the tide condescended to turn. I motored the last three miles dead into the wind instead of tacking.

It was getting late, and I worried I might not make it back to my mooring in time to catch the launch. Our launch service stops operation at seven o'clock. I suppose her skipper needs to eat by then. Mariners no longer fare on wormy hardtack and stale water or work thirty hours a day—they expect their creature comforts and deserve them. They also need a respite from my fantastic fabrications.

It's taken me only a couple of seasons to put at least three launch drivers out of commission. My tales of Sylphs and sea serpents, and my revelations concerning the Race Rock Monster, have caused these erstwhile stalwarts to hide in the ship's store every time I call in on 68.

And finding a copy of my *Journals of Constant Waterman* in plain sight on the bench in the launch where any innocent mariner might peruse it and be corrupted has been the incentive for me to repair my Whitehall and get her back in the water as quickly as possible.

The Race

Yesterday I went out to play aboard *Moon Wind*.

"Bit of a breeze out there," the launch driver said.

I could see the flag at the head of the inner cove snapping; see the whitecaps awaiting me farther out. When it's fifteen, gusting to twenty, why bother with a jib? The smallest I own is a 120. I just wasn't in the mood for fighting the helm. I took a single reef in the main, started the motor for just in case, and cast off my mooring pendant.

I quickly zipped between the moored boats, came about, and headed out to the sound. The breeze was out of the NNW; the tide ran with me but soon would change. I traipsed along at three knots; I hardly heeled at all. I supposed I could shake out the reef in my main. Some of the many boats on the sound were under mainsail alone. Some had taken a reef. Some of them had full press of sail. Farther out, a couple of big boats flew brightly colored spinnakers. Having an ample waterline and a crew makes all the difference.

While I was absorbing all this data, I felt the first puff. Being reefed down, it scarcely heeled me over twenty degrees. The two-foot chop was not a nuisance at all. I left my main reefed and headed out to the Race. The Race is that five-mile gap between Long Island and Fishers Island. It's the eastern mouth of Long Island Sound, and the ocean can be quite busy fitting through it. What makes it fun is that the reef spans the breadth of the Race. It averages eighty feet in depth, but the waters on either side are three times that. When the water is in a hurry, some of it tends to go up and down a bit. Near Orient Point the current can reach five knots.

What a perfect place to play on a little boat on a breezy day. By the time I reached the Race, the chop was four feet and the water exceptionally wet. By the time I passed Valiant Rock and neared the lighthouse, the chop was five feet. The waves could not agree on one direction; the period between them rather diminished. Little *MoonWind* rolled and pitched and plunged and bucked. Oh yes; she yawed just a trifle, too. I had my hands full meeting each wave at such an angle as not to entirely drench me. At this I was quite successful, most of the time. The wind, of course, contributed what it could. I was glad it seldom exceeded twenty knots.

After a half hour of this, with limited forward progress, it occurred to me that, ahead, the seas seemed worse. I never worried that the waves would capsize my boat. I never worried that I might be flung to the fishes. I only worried that all that spray was dulling the brightwork on which I'd lavished varnish. Why go to all that trouble to have your brightwork crusted with salt?

I thought perhaps it was time to come about. There wasn't a proper gap between the waves. I waited until what seemed a propitious interval and put the helm down, hard. *MoonWind* staggered into the wind, but stalled and then fell off. I regained steerageway. My second attempt, I came up gradually, but couldn't get her quite to cross the wind. While I attempted to back the main, the chop slued me about. It wasn't quite rough enough to bury her bow; for that I was grateful.

I determined to jibe her before it grew any worse. The trick was to keep my footing. Falling across the cockpit would not facilitate maneuvers. Hip against the tiller, both hands trimming the main, one foot braced on the locker, all I saw was water; then all I saw was sky.

I jibed her without a problem. I even escaped some rope burn as the mainsheet flew through my hand. Amazing how warm, how quickly, that mainsheet gets. It's similar to picking up a hot ember off the hearth to toss back on the fire. You know you'll have but a moment to enjoy the glad sensation.

In twenty minutes, I could feel the diminution of the chop. But the tide was still determined to get through the Race, despite my advice. For another hour, I porpoised amid a moderate sea; the wind had abated some. Eventually, I wafted back to West Cove at a rousing two knots, too complacent even to shake out my reef. The occasional puffs proved no inconvenience, whatever.

I picked up my mooring pendant and squared things away. The launch appeared just as I fit my drop boards into their slot.

"Find any wind?" the launch driver asked.

"Not close by," I replied. "But I went to the Race and found they'd saved me a capful." I balanced on my toe rail, then hopped aboard the launch.

"What's that crusty stuff all over your glasses?" the driver queried.

"Oh, that," I replied. "That's from sticking my face in the sea to console the barnacles on my rudder for disturbing their afternoon nap."

"In that case," he said, as he brought the launch round the breakwater, "I needn't be bothered to tell you to go soak your head."

Rail down

Mason's Island

There's a cove on the east side of Mason's Island about a mile deep and a third of that in width. Mason's Island forms the east bank of Mystic Harbor, and at its northern extreme, joins the mainland by a causeway. The cove abruptly meets the old Post Road and constricts to a humble estuary that passes beneath it. To the east of the cove are two young islands and bits of marsh sprinkled with boulders. There'll be a cartography quiz on all of the above first thing Friday morning.

Now for your next lesson. Sit up straight and don't fidget, *Moon-Wind,* else you'll have to stand in the corner again. There's a good girl.

A monstrous seawall defines St. Edmund's Retreat on Enders Island, connected to the tip of Mason's Island by a causeway. Two nuns lean to the current at the cove's mouth just opposite the retreat. This seems fitting. Keep away from the nun nearest St. Edmunds; her habit is rather stony and inhospitable.

Just above St. Edmunds lies Mason's Island Yacht Club. They tend a few dozen moorings, the last of which lies halfway up the cove. Above that the water shoals.

"Plenty of water," said our friends aboard *Tara.* "And good bottom and ample shelter from this north wind."

I hove to at the mouth of the cove, dropped my sails, and motored up into the wind. I paid my respects to the two nuns and proceeded through the mooring field to *Tara,* snug on her hook in seven feet of water. We rafted with her, then kedged out an anchor as an afterthought.

We settled in for a lovely evening. The cove lay placid about us; the wind diminished; the stars proliferated. We slathered butter on king crab legs and fresh-picked corn and agreed that life was worth living.

After supper, we sat on *Tara's* broad stern rail and fed little fish with crab scraps. Until some larger fish came by and had to spoil their party.

Now it's half past six on Sunday morning and I'm guarding a mug of French roast in my cockpit. It cooled off to fifty or less last night and made us grateful we had a blanket to fight for. There's a touch of autumn already this Labor Day weekend. The air is crisp. You could easily stretch and stroke those soft green woods on Fishers Island, three miles away. The dolorous whistle at Latimer Reef, downwind and around the bend, easily carries this far. The flags ashore are beginning to lift; a sail inches up the sound; a scatter of ducks quick-wings it toward the marshes. A halyard on a moored sloop nearby raps out a jangly message to the morning.

Sailing through Fishers Island Sound a few hours later, the tiller breaks off in my hand. Fortunately, the breeze and sea are gentle. I motor sail the two miles back to our mooring, steering with the outboard. As long as I go only forward, the rudder waggles like the tail of a trout who's merely holding her own in a slow-moving stream.

The launch driver looks at my tiller and shakes his head.

"Lucky it wasn't blowing like it did the week before last," he says.

Only too true; I was rail down that weekend.

Back at the boat shop, I find a length of ash of perfect cross section and only need to shave the two faces with the table saw to fit the tiller housing. I transfer the three bolt holes, run my router around the tiller to radius the edges, and sand it smooth. A thirty-minute tiller. Back aboard *MoonWind*, I bolt the tiller to the rudder head, raise our sails, and flutter back out to the sound. The westering sun glitters upon the ripples on our port bow as we make our way to Pine Island.

Again we raft with *Tara* by Bushy Point. This time, there's scarcely water to spare. As the tide runs out, our two boats slowly swing closer to Bushy Point. By nightfall, *MoonWind*'s keel has found the mud. The wind picks up, but our two craft can't respond. *Tara*, with her two huge inboards, can't break *MoonWind* free.

But the tide has turned. At half past twelve, we begin to swing into the wind. We motor out to deeper water and reset both our anchors. It's half past one before I hit the sack.

At half past six the gleeful sun demands I make the coffee.

175

A Seagull in the Varnish

Went out for a sail last Sunday and discovered breeze enough to share with numerous boats. I couldn't be bothered to take a reef, so had to suffer the indignity of heeling over thirty degrees for much of the afternoon.

The tide and wind had a disagreement, as usual, about the preferred direction of the sea. Consequently, it proved a mite choppy, but not enough to don foul-weather gear. A delightful afternoon immediately followed. It's finally come to that time of year when abundant wind is available by the bagful; when fifteen knots can be found without much searching.

Earlier this week, I was varnishing rails on a Dyer 29 docked in her slip. The air felt balmy and dry for a change, and the breeze dried the varnish in minutes.

An obvious sailor (he had a gray beard and a six-inch ring in his ear) sauntered down the pier, whistling a chantey and twirling his marlinspike.

"Lovely day for a sail," I suggested.

"Good day to drown, you mean," he observed. "It's blowing a steady twenty-eight knots."

"I suppose I'd allow you a reef or two," I replied.

"There's a seagull stuck in your varnish," he observed.

You know the type: always changes the subject when it proves inconvenient to lie. I've never yet found that to be a particular problem. Besides, it was too good a drying day to waste it sailing: I managed to lavish fourteen coats on that Dyer in forty minutes. This time of year, varnishing vessels outdoors is problematic. Some days you need to hold an umbrella over the teak that you varnish.

I'm hoping there'll be some work indoors before the snow gets too far over my knees. Otherwise, I'll be forced to stay at home and write more journals. Just now I'm busy scheduling book signings. I'm making the rounds of libraries, bookshops, and cafés nearby Noank. I've limited my driving to an hour in every direction. At least I had until I was reintroduced to Bunch of Grapes in Vineyard Haven. I first went there a year ago aboard *MoonWind*. It's a lovely bookshop located in the center of the village. They emailed me and asked if I'd like to read there this autumn.

I immediately laid out a rhumb line to the bookstore. Fifty miles to Cuttyhunk the first day. The next day cut through Canapitsit Channel, breeze up Vineyard Sound a dozen miles, then chase the ferry 'round West Chop and into the village harbor.

"Ferry," I mused. "Alternative methods of travel."

A dim bulb lighted in the murk between my ears. I could drive to New Bedford and avail myself of public transportation. Instead of towing my Whitehall seventy miles and rowing ashore through the chop from a transient mooring, I could disembark with the quality from a huge, impeccable vessel; saunter down the gangway with a studied nonchalance; straighten my paisley silk ascot; hail a cab with a wave of my cane; and be driven the last three blocks to Bunch of Grapes.

It's true I wouldn't be nearly so salty as I'd get sailing in on *MoonWind*. This time of year, my beard tends to get a bit caked with spray and it takes my mermaid an hour to comb it out. I'd be able to swagger, or stagger, or whatever sailors purport to do after riding a plunging vessel for months and months or maybe even a weekend.

I have to decide what image I ought to portray: unwashed, salty dog or debonair author. In either case, I need to remember to leave my slimy sea boots outside the door.

Thanksgiving 2007

Yesterday was Thanksgiving. What better way to thank this world for its many blessings than go out to greet the wind, fondle the sea, round an island, be kissed by a sunbeam?

High fifties and sunny, bleated the weather clown. For once he was right. Ten to fifteen knots, promised the wind-watcher. Right again. Furtive sunbeams playing amid the fleecy skies, they agreed. Right for a total of three out of three. Amazing!

I packed some lunch, buttoned up my long johns, and called my crew. At half past nine I hanked on my 120 headsail, unsnapped my boom cover. Here came my crew—bright-eyed with anticipation. I primed my outboard motor and started it up. The crew cast off and I backed *Moon Wind* slowly out of her slip. The breeze had not yet built and, within the breakwater, all lay placid. I shifted into forward and motored out to the channel.

My plan was to head to the Race, follow the easterly ebb of the tide down the backside of Fishers Island, cut through Wicopesset Pass, and come home through Fishers Island Sound. Just less than twenty miles, all told, with a lovely breeze out of the south-southwest to move me.

Except for the first five miles out to the Race. These would be directly into the wind. And tacking to get there and fighting the tide would add at least an hour to the venture. I left the sails secured and motored the first five miles into the wind. After all, our wives expected us home by four o'clock. Some sort of special dinner, we were given to understand.

We cut between the Dumplings, dodged a few dozen colorful lobster pot buoys, and approached Race Rock. Here stands a rugged granite lighthouse, dating from 1873. We passed outboard of the Rock and met the Race. When two hundred feet of water pass over an eighty-foot reef, some of that water climbs on its neighbor's back for a better view. Today was not too bad—merely a three-foot chop from three directions.

MoonWind practiced some bouncing and cavorting. She bucked, she pranced, she kicked her little heels in the air. I worried she might inadvertently throw a shoe. After we'd passed through the worst of the chop, I went below to square a few things away. Through the ports, I could see the horizon dip and rise and plunge and disappear. After ten minutes, my stomach followed suit. I raced for the cockpit and decorated *MoonWind*'s lathered flank.

In six minutes' time, I felt well enough to shake out the reef in my mainsail and haul it up. I set my preventer, hoisted the jib, and off we flew on a very broad reach toward the east. By this time we were several miles off the sea side of Fishers Island. We sped its six-mile length in less than an hour. Not bad for a boat with a hull speed of just six knots.

The wind had picked up a trifle as we jibed and set a course for the pass at Wicopesset. I headed athwart the wind and sea and bore up against them both. We tore a track through the rolling tide and, in less than an hour, shoved through the pass without incident, rounded buoy 13 by Latimer Reef, and headed up for our single tack back to Noank.

Aside from a few small powerboats that were fishing for Thanksgiving dinner, we had the sea to ourselves. At journey's end we spied a sloop that motored into the mouth of Mystic Harbor—but we hadn't glimpsed her sail all afternoon.

Apparently, it was much too gorgeous a day for the common sailor. Given the choice between black-backed gull and turkey, he chose the turkey. Given the choice between watching the sea plunge 'round the point and watching the fullback plunge for another yard, he chose the fullback. Given the choice between a warm southerly breeze and forced hot air, he chose the forced hot air.

We had nearly the whole of the wholesome sea to ourselves. It was one more thing to be truly thankful for.

Annoying the Seals

Well, we're getting a bit of sugaring weather here in southern Connecticut. You know what I mean. Nights below freezing, sunny days with temperatures high in the forties. Makes the sap in the sugar maples feel its oats so it wants to climb to the uppermost twigs for a better view of the world. All you need do is stand nearby with a sap bucket and make promises of little girls eating pancakes, and that sap will get so excited it'll leap into your bucket. For every quart of sap, you'll get an ounce of syrup. All you need do is take your truck up to the back forty and bring in a few cords of wood to keep that sap seething and steaming until it's reduced.

But I wasn't about to tell you how I filled my canoe and bathtub with maple sap while I boiled more on my wood range all day and all night until I needed to open my doors and windows to let out the steam. And how I made so much maple syrup I was able to swap a gallon to a New York book reviewer for a half dozen books of new poetry, and gave away whole gallons for Christmas presents. Or how I fed my tomcat maple milk until he could scarcely drag his sagging belly across the kitchen.

I thought today I'd tell you about the seals, and about the lovely slant of winter sunlight across the sound, and the distant purr of the lobster boats as they harvested their catch.

It all began (as the spinners of tales so often quaintly put it) when I rose from my little bed early one Sunday morning. It was still below freezing. I built up the fire in the woodstove, and stalked about the house in my long johns, thinking about the weather report that lurked on my computer. I checked it again. High of forty-eight; breeze west-southwest at six to eight knots. I checked the thermometer outside the kitchen window. Twenty-six degrees. Warm for February, but nowhere near warm enough to tempt me to play on the water. That windchill factor is what does watermen in.

By eleven o'clock, it exceeded forty. I went out to bring in wood and sniffed the air. I looked about the snow-free yard in the hope of glimpsing a crocus. I faced the sun and felt its benevolence smooth the cares from my brow.

By twelve o'clock it was forty-five. I vaulted into my pickup truck and trundled down to the boatyard. I peeled off my cockpit cover and tossed it down below. I unsnapped my boom cover, started my motor, hanked on a working jib. I cast off my lines and backed *MoonWind* out of her slip, turned and puttered into the channel and by all the finger piers. A couple working on their boat looked up as I passed.

I imagined them saying to each other, "Where does he think he's going? It's only February!"

"I'm off to annoy the seals," I should have replied.

Beyond the breakwater, beyond the mooring field, I raised my sails. I turned off my motor, trimmed my jib, and settled down, basking in the vast and voluptuous quiet.

The harbor seals were busy awaiting me on Middle Clump. The tide was low and the rocks well proud of the water. A dozen seals, as many cormorants, and numerous herring gulls were busy holding down the rocks to keep them from floating away.

I wafted slowly closer, the breeze on my quarter. At a hundred yards, some of the seals abruptly abandoned ship. Others waited until I had halved that distance. At twenty yards, the last seal reluctantly rolled into the sound. The birds had departed. Several sleek heads bobbed nearby in the water. As I passed downwind of Middle Clump, a fragrance assailed my nostrils. Imagine wearing a respirator with an old, old fishing trawler stuck inside it. One good whiff and I started to blow on the sails. Whew! Hope I never come back as a polar bear. Eating seals is something I wouldn't fancy.

But I'm sure that seals find one another attractive. At least once during the year. I can picture lady seals rubbing themselves with ripened mullet to attract more gentleman seals. Personally, I'd just as soon play in a barrel of lobster bait.

Being satisfied that our seals were healthy and nourished, I wended the numerous lobster pot buoys and zigged across the sound. A couple of lobster boats hauled their traps. The breeze consented to keep me moving at two to three knots. The descending sun spread its richness across the stippled water. In the distance, the pointillistic ferry to Orient Point departed the Thames and flowed across the flood tide to Sag Harbor.

At four o'clock, I motored *MoonWind* gently into her slip and made her fast. Then I dashed home and wrote about the curvaceous mermaids sunning their lovely selves on Middle Clump.

Little Narragansett Bay

Having spent September and October rebuilding *MoonWind*'s deck-house, I wondered if I should need remedial sailing lessons before I ventured forth. *MoonWind* looked at me coyly and winked her eye.

"Come with me, sailor," she said.

So off I went with her to find some breeze. I remembered how to furl the anchor and oil the relative bearing and actually hanked the mainsail onto the backstay all by myself. Beyond that, all was instinctual, and me and *MoonWind* cruised downwind most of this lovely day. I even remembered to rig my preventer. We made four knots from Avery Point to Watch Hill, Rhode Island, changing course by shifting the genny from starboard to port and back to starboard again to neatly avoid running down Fishers Island. It would be a shame to sink it. At a mere six miles long, Fishers Island presents a challenge to *MoonWind* when she gets that gleam in her eye.

By judicious tacking, we also avoided both East and Middle Clumps as well as Johnson's Rock and the Seal Rocks. We also refrained from climbing aboard several fishing boats anchored off Latimer Reef. We made it through Watch Hill Passage by scaring several score of dozing eiders, and emerged into open water by half past lunch. This consisted of strips of dried papaya and shelled pecans. We took time out from this veritable feast to wave to the lighthouse keeper at Watch Hill. This notable worthy spends his frenetic days and nights swapping red and white lightbulbs every two seconds in order to alert us to the vagaries of Rhode Island. For us Connecticut folks these prove considerable. Why, Rhode Islanders haven't even learned to add cream to their clam chowdah. Everyone knows that the threat of cholesterol adds a certain zest to the taste of clams.

By two o'clock, we still had fifteen miles to traverse to reach Point

Judith and the wind diminished until we made just three knots. Since they messed with the clocks again and made it get dark before the sun has clambered over the yardarm, we wouldn't make it to Harbor of Refuge until well after dark. Then we'd have a mile and a half of narrow channel to navigate to our wonted anchorage back of Gardiner Island. I'm normally not afraid of the dark—as long as there aren't any trolls—but folks have a way of leaving things out in the channels hereabouts, like lobster pots and logs, and numerous unlighted threats to navigation. *MoonWind* has a fondness for lobster pot buoys; she sheared the bushing on our outboard just last summer by catching one between her prop and the trim tab.

So I came about and made my way back to Watch Hill. We rounded Napatree Point and headed for Stonington Borough. Sure enough, the first quarter mile of the narrow channel leading behind Watch Hill was clogged with lobster pot buoys. Navigating this part of the world in the dark can be a challenge. The lobsters lurk in the channels in the hope of waylaying small sailboats and eating their crews.

Having slalomed my way to Sandy Point, I wended the mile-long channel, hung a right at nun 22, and let go my twenty-pound plow anchor in nine feet of cool, dark water on the backside of Napatree Point by the entrance to Watch Hill Harbor. I backed down with the motor to set my hook, then squared away in time to admire the streaked vermillion sky. I had the mile of anchorage all to myself. I then set about attacking my provisions. Replete at last, I washed my dishes, lit my masthead anchor light, and took my pen in hand . . .

Next morning the water sustained scarcely a ripple, though I heard the sea rasping the seaward shore of Napatree Point. The night was uneventful. No revelers, no drifting boats, no ice-cream-crazed children driving rubber dinghies at full tilt. November is a time for introspection and, when I looked inside, I found there a distinct request for breakfast. I drank my coffee huddled at my table, for the dew was a half inch deep on the cockpit seats. My breath steamed up my newly rebuilt port lights, and I heard the penguins breaking the ice in my toilet.

Actually, I exaggerate—it never got much below forty degrees. I made a hardy breakfast of baked beans and toast. By noontime it was sixty. I shed a layer of clothing and got under way. I ascended the Pawcatuck River back of Watch Hill under power, for wind was scarce and the channel mostly narrow. After a mile, the channel grew narrower still, and my GPS showed only a teaspoon of water outside the markers. I came about and descended the sluggish stream.

The breeze picked up by the time I made it out to Stonington Point, and I hoisted my rags and made it the ten miles home on just one tack. The sizable motor yacht *Amazon* overtook me off Ram Island. Even under power, her sails furled, she looked impressive; a huge British flag—large enough to cover *MoonWind* from pulpit to taffrail—rippled from her stern sheets. She crossed my bows and ascended the Mystic River. I guessed Mystic Seaport to be her destination. Aside from a few fishermen, only a couple of sails graced the sound.

I made it home with breeze to spare and sauntered into my slip.

POINT JUDITH POND

Narragansett Towers, Narragansett, Rhode Island

Indigo to Amber

From sheltered Noank, Connecticut to Harbor of Refuge, just this side of wicked Point Judith, Rhode Island, is only twenty-three miles as the herring gull wings her way. My yew-green *Moon Wind* knows the way so well by now that she'd blithely venture there by herself were she not well tethered to her mooring most of the time.

With wind and tide at my back I make good time; my two sails spread to trap the ample breeze. I keep within a mile of shore, and glimpse a half dozen harbor seals basking on the reef by Wicopesset.

By half past four, I approach the heaped stone seawall that circles the mile-wide, nearly round Harbor of Refuge. Without the wall, the waters mount as the heaving tides from Narragansett grapple the impatient sea.

I sheet in my sails and surge amid the chest-high waves and through the great gate in the seawall. A channel wends between two jetties into Point Judith Pond. This is a salt pond three miles long and, in places, nearly a mile in breadth. I waft by the fishing fleet at its piers, by the ferry slips, the dockside restaurants, the small marinas. I flutter the channel halfway up the placid pond, where modest summerhouses flank the shore; I round little, uninhabited Gardiner Island and drop my anchor.

I douse my sails, stow my gear, descend the companionway to my cabin, and put on the kettle. By six o'clock, I'm ensconced in my cockpit, cherishing green tea. The sun dips slowly into the distant ocean. The broad pond passes from indigo to amber edged with pewter. I perch with my notebook on my knee and recount the half dozen mermaids I saw basking on the reef by Wicopesset.

Blowing on the Sails

Here, behind Gardiner Island in placid Point Judith Pond, it is partially overcast yet pleasant. Birdsong and breeze, two gulls on the pebbly beach discussing breakfast, seven sloops at anchor nearby, some with their anchor lights still awink in the dawn.

Cast off my mooring pendant at Noank at nearly noon, yesterday, with my 150 genoa hoisted, and wafted out to the sound. Wind was north-northwesterly at maybe eight knots. Even against the tide I made three knots. The breeze seemed fresher farther out as I reached down Fishers Island Sound toward Watch Hill. Soon I managed four knots.

Well, I thought, this suffices. Four knots with headsail alone, and when the tide relaxes a bit and when I pass Watch Hill I'll have all the wind I want for a pleasant reach down the shore to Point Judith. Of course, I said this aloud, and Someone was listening.

I passed the stubby lighthouse at Latimer Reef with its mournful horn as the breeze began to recede. Slower and yet more slowly did *MoonWind* nose her way toward Watch Hill Point. Now I should raise the main, thought I, and then that wind went foul. It all but ceased; it spun my wind vane 'round and back and about; it died completely.

It was half past two; I had sixteen miles to go. Not counting another mile and a half up the pond to my anchorage. For fifteen minutes, my genoa slatted from side to side and embraced my mast with unexpected passion. Then the breeze settled down and slowly emitted a series of muffled yawns out of the southeast. I hoisted my main and soon attained a rousing three knots. For about an hour.

By four o'clock I made but 2.3 knots by blowing hard on my sails. The tide had changed in my favor but I had a dozen miles and more to go. I started my motor.

I know you purists scoff at internal combustion. Unfortunately, scoff as hard as I might, I went no faster. Perhaps my method of scoffing needs improvement. If there'd been another anchorage in the vicinity, I could have made for it, but there's nothing here but sandy beach for fifteen miles with nothing to block the wind from the south except the far-flung isle of Hispaniola. The thought of supper at midnight at Point Judith decided me. Crackers and cheese and raisins are all very well, but fighting the helm in a four-knot gale gives a sailor an appetite. I started my motor. What with the tide, that wind, and my motor, I soon exceeded five knots.

As I busily garnished a raisin for afternoon tea, I suddenly looked around—I do this occasionally—and startled to see a series of five-foot waves with angry crests approaching me broadside—from the beach! I carefully swaddled my little raisin, tenderly laid it among its brothers and sisters back in their box, and leapt for the helm. I prepared to be boarded by the first piratical wave.

Here they came. Three waves, but a couple of seconds apart, crashed into me. *MoonWind* casually rolled a bit and showed them her naked flank. This embarrassed those waves no end. They covered their eyes and scuttled off, roaring to one another. *MoonWind* rocked so gently that those raisins all fell asleep.

Don't ask me where three such presumptuous waves originated. The shore, a mile and more away, is too gradual to make the seas rebound. Besides, the eight-inch swells had scarcely the inclination to go ashore. There wasn't a vessel nearby to throw such a wake.

The waves were scarcely a mile in length. They never recurred. I can only guess that Poseidon had spanked one of his saucier mermaids.

Off Point Judith, the swells ran merely three feet. This, for Point Judith, represents a dead calm. I tucked within the seawall just ahead of the Block Island ferry and doused my sails. The channel up Point Judith Pond is narrow and filled with boats. I motored in beside one ferry as another ferry emerged. I ascended the channel beyond the ferry landing in the company of two skiffs.

By the time I rounded Gardiner Island, the sun was low in the sky. I stopped just shy of two white, well-fed sloops and dropped my Danforth. I let out my thirty feet of clean new chain and forty feet of roding. I backed down till my little motor complained, then shut it off. Ahh—the quiet. By the time I squared away it was time for supper.

I knew this for a fact, for one of the local swans came by to remind me.

The Sea, the Breeze, the Sky

Waking on Point Judith Pond is always a pleasure; its serenity whelms my senses. The light was diffuse, the water a silvery shimmer. After a leisurely breakfast consisting of French roast, a notebook, and a pencil, I got under way.

As soon as I rounded Gardiner Island, I shut off my motor and ran before the wind with only my genny down the mile-long channel. Past the various private anchorages, past the two quahoggers wading past their waists, past the boatyards, past the ferry slips and the rust-streaked fishing fleet. Beyond the jetties, I hove to in the outer harbor, washed and stowed my muddy chain, raised my mainsail, and set a course for Connecticut.

The wind was mild but the tide ran in my direction. Two to three knots before the wind brought me back to Watch Hill. Beyond lies Fishers Island Sound: Connecticut on the northern shore, Fishers Island, New York to the south. Twenty square miles of sound provide a playground for numerous boats, many of which continue out to sea. There is scarcely any commercial traffic except a very occasional dragger and the scurrying, fragrant lobster boats that tend their strings of pots.

Within the sound, the wind picked up until I made four knots. I dropped my sails a quarter mile from my mooring and motored in. The stern of the boat moored just upwind of me swung no more than a boat length beyond my pendant. Consequently, I couldn't pass my mooring whip and grab it from the cockpit, but had to scuttle forward and leave the helm. As soon as you leave the helm, the wind turns your bow, and you find yourself leaning far over the pulpit, gesticulating with your boat hook, and exercising expletives that your mother never taught you. It is only by exercise that you keep them limber.

Nevertheless, both mooring pendants eventually made it aboard. I scrubbed and sluiced the pond mud from my foredeck, stowed my jib, and covered my main. I roused the harbor launch on my VHF and practiced my latest lies on the credulous launch driver.

Another weekend of sailing has come to a close. Another fifty miles and fifteen hours of scooping breeze from the sky. Another journal; another record of thoughts, ideas, impressions. Half the reason we venture forth is to talk about it afterward. The thrill of the chase proves only the merest beginning.

My publisher has sent my book to the printer. My new covers, front and back, have miraculously appeared upon my website. Amazon shows my unavailable journals—already discounted. I'm compiling contacts for reading and selling books. Perhaps I shall eventually earn enough by writing not to have to clamber about in other sailors' boats, scraping and sanding and inhaling dust and solvents. Life is precious, precarious, and the sea extremely inviting.

I have no intention of crossing the sea; there is coastline enough on this side of North America to keep me amused for years. Amused in the sense of inspired. I think I can also amuse, or regale, my readers a good while yet.

It may not be too late to become the constant waterman I've dreamed of being all these too-dry decades. From an errant boy with a leaky skiff on the river, I've become an errant old man with a sailing boat on the sound. Aside from loss of hair on my head and proliferation of fur about my chin, the changes of a half century appear negligible. I've become an old gray water rat, indeed.

I used to take my fishing reel apart and clean it occasionally when I was a lad. Now I have a sailboat to clean. I used to slop paint on my dinghy once a season. Now I carefully lavish varnish on my Whitehall pulling boat and her slim spruce oars. I don't mind the chores so much as the carking responsibilities. Working at tedious jobs to pay tedious bills only wastes my quickly diminishing years. And who has time to waste? This world whirs urgently by, whirs urgently by, and the sea, the breeze, the sky are about us, waiting.

NARRAGANSETT BAY

WICKFORD HARBOR LIGHT
1882–1930

The Usual Surge and Four-Foot Chop

Here I am again at Point Judith Pond, my home away from West Cove, swinging on my brand-new, twenty-pound Hydrobubble anchor that arrived just the day before yesterday.

I snuck *Moon Wind* into a slip afternoon before last to work on her and provision her before departing for Narragansett Bay. Pulled out the holding tank and scrubbed both it and the fo'c'sle.

I then installed two new dome lights, one of them over the galley. This now precludes my being quite so careless preparing what I eat, but my stomach has yet to thank me. Perhaps the thank-you card got lost in the mail. There's a bit of that going around these days.

I also rigged my new anchor and adjusted the chain stopper. Filled my water tank and hosed down the deck. Stowed enough food and clothing for my coming week away, and generally squared away everything so thoroughly that I'm hard-pressed to find rounded corners anywhere.

By the following morning all was done and I set sail toward the east. The tide would be against me all afternoon, but what of that? A ten-knot southerly breeze on my beam kept me full and by at four knots, and the three-foot swells sufficed to keep me awake. As the sun reclined, I blew into Harbor of Refuge at Point Judith, headed up and dropped my main. With the wind dead astern, I let my headsail pull me up the channel to this anchorage.

Two motor cruisers are anchored here—my only neighbors. This anchorage could accommodate a half hundred boats of a fathom's draft. The south wind comes straight up the pond the entire night and swings me to and fro, but with a scope of eight to one, I don't bounce a bit.

This morning, clouds prevail. The sun keeps shoving the clouds aside, but they, in turn, shove back. Ten to fifteen knots, says NOAA, sometimes gusting to twenty. Later today, sometimes gusting to thirty. As soon as I have my breakfast, I should weigh anchor. I hope to be secure in Greenwich Harbor by afternoon. My friends will be there on their Uniflight 42. Hopefully I can raft alongside as she's parked at the end of the pier.

I leave Point Judith Pond bright and early at ten. Perhaps neither early nor especially bright. My thirty feet of anchor chain drips mud and I haven't time to clean it, so I pile it with my anchor on the foredeck. On my way out past the jetties I meet two men returning in a skiff.

"Rough out there!" hollers one of them.

I nod vigorously twice to let him know I understand. But Harbor of Refuge isn't all that lumpy. I hoist my smaller jib and single-reefed main and head for the breach in the seawall. I sluice off my chain and anchor and stow them while *Moon Wind* sails herself. Just outside the breachway, I encounter the usual surge and four-foot chop and lack of consideration of the sea, but nothing to become alarmed about. I buck out past the big red bell and fall off to round Point Judith. By the time I pass the occulting light in the lighthouse on the point, the sea subsides.

Narragansett Bay has three mouths. The westerly lies between the town of Narragansett, on the mainland, and Jamestown, on Conanicut Island. The second mouth parts Conanicut from Aquidneck: that island most famous for housing the town of Newport. To the east runs the Sakonnet River, then the mainland again. The first town you encounter is Little Compton. Beyond, farther east, spread the wilds of Massachusetts.

People aver that it's safe to travel there, but I don't know. I drove as far as New Bedford once and their streets were all one way. Had to come home to Connecticut via Vermont. Their harbor was populated by large wet fish in heaps aboard large wet boats. Their creamy chowder had not only quahogs but cod and scallops in it. It wasn't a proper chowder at all, and I left the restaurant highly disappointed. They had the nerve to charge me for a second helping.

I head for the lighthouse on Beavertail—the southern tip of Conanicut Island—and cut between it and the rocks off Narragansett. Upon these rocks stands the ruined foundation of a steel-reinforced tower—Whale Rock Lighthouse—swept away with its keeper during the 1938 Hurricane.

I head up, drop my mainsail, and waft up the bay with my genoa billowed nobly by the breeze. I have all afternoon to make twenty miles, and I settle back on my La-Z-Boy recliner with my lunch.

BEAVERTAIL LIGHT 1856
CONANICUT ISLAND
NARRAGANSETT BAY
RHODE ISLAND

Greenwich Bay

Coming up Narragansett Bay at a comfortable four knots, I approach Dutch Island to starboard. Behind this wooded eighty-one acres lies a lovely, sheltered harbor. On the foot of Dutch, the forty-two-foot lighthouse, dating from 1857, undergoes restoration.

I pass beneath the simple span that connects North Kingstown with Jamestown. I say "simple" for it has no towers, no cables, no visible trusses; merely a single bare sweep of steel that connects several tall piers. The centermost span bridges six hundred feet; the girders hover a hundred feet above little *MoonWind*'s mast. The pedestal for each massive pier is the size of a summer cottage. Unfortunately, after they constructed this work of art, people presumed it functional and now insist on driving their vehicles over it.

North of Conanicut Island lies Prudence Island, four miles long. Nearby are Hope and Patience Islands, designated estuarine sanctuaries. I looked for Faith and Charity, but Rhode Island, apparently, ran out of islands before she ran out of virtues.

Just above Prudence juts Warwick Neck, a part of the mainland. Here I hang a left—as we sailors say—and enter Greenwich Bay. Someone, long since, discovered its inner reaches conducive to mooring numerous boats. The cormorants, also long since, discovered the mummichogs here extremely friendly.

Captain Uniflight's cruiser lies at the end of the first pier beyond the first mooring field in East Greenwich. I drop my jib and motor up gently alongside. The breeze obliges by keeping us apart. I make fast, adjust my fenders, and try to make both *MoonWind* and me presentable. She has the advantage of being better looking to begin with.

Captain Uniflight shows up about nightfall, and we spend an hour throwing books and crackers at each other. By the time Madam Uniflight arrives, we're ready for supper. It's fortunate that she finds us both amusing.

Next morning, as they both have to work, I climb the hill to Main Street and have a delightful breakfast at Jigger's Diner. This is an old-fashioned diner from 1950 that stands end-on to the street. You climb three steps, open the door, and find yourself wedged between the antique cash register and the trim, vivacious waitress.

At ten o'clock Saturday morning they're quite busy, but I wait only minutes for a seat at the counter. Three dozen people put themselves outside French toast with strawberries, corned beef hash, sizzling steak, and poached eggs. A peck of home-fried potatoes adorns the grill; their fragrance vies with that of the fresh-brewed coffee. I have an omelet crammed with roasted vegetables and a helping of perfect home fries. A steaming mug of coffee and crisp rye toast completes the treatment.

Replete, I stagger outside and meet the glare of the sun. I proceed to amble until the potatoes and eggs are best distributed. Then I slide down the hillside to the harbor and admire boats.

After noon, Madam Uniflight returns and we give our kayaks a chance to play in the water. Her sea kayak tracks well through the gentle chop and breeze; my stubby little flat-water boat bounces and splashes and wriggles. She has to wait up for me every fifteen minutes. It certainly curbs my garrulity to be so far apart. On the other hand, I have fifteen minutes to think of extremely clever things to say. We round Potowomut Neck and ascend the estuary. But we started late, and Captain and Madam Uniflight expect people for drinks. We decide to curtail our adventure, and just mess around the salt marsh by the mouth of the estuary. We admire a rank of cormorants drying themselves on a ruinous wall; we scrape our bottoms amid the stands of grasses.

Then we return. After six miles of tide and breeze, I'm ready for almost anything; namely, a nap. I hose off my kayak and stow her back on deck. The time has come to say good-bye to my friends and take my leave, but first they kindly offer me a shower. Imagine that: a shower aboard a boat. You turn the knob, and voilà: Hot water comes out! What won't they think of next?

Those of us with showerless boats ought to get one of those black plastic bags that you drape on your boom to heat five gallons of water by solar power. Then you prance, naked, in your cockpit, to the delight of all old ladies with binoculars, and rinse the salt from your bristles. In the winter you can use this water to create a small skating rink. You can whiz about your cockpit, and use your unshipped tiller to practice your slap shot.

After my ablutions, I bid my friends adieu. As evening approaches I opt to motor merely a mile to Potowomut Neck. This bight in the shore, just off the state park, provides a good anchorage. I drop my hook by the prettiest little Bristol I've ever seen and settle in for the night.

PLUM BEACH LIGHT 1899
NARRAGANSETT BAY
RHODE ISLAND

Potowomut Neck

This morning I exchange salutations with *White Dove*'s skipper. He confirms what my weather station predicted: light air only all of today and tomorrow. Just now my weather vane flops between south and north, with occasional forays into other departments. The tide licks gently at the fringe of waterline growth on *Moon Wind*. I could haul my hook and still be here in an hour.

A heavy shower accosts us for fifteen minutes accompanied by a roaring half-knot gale. I'm reminded that my mast boot needs replacing. Following this, the Bristol weighs her anchor and motors away. Time I did the same.

Under way with only my motor, my chart book on my lap. The passage between Patience and Prudence Islands has seven feet of water—about in the center, sort of; more or less—but no sign of markers. It rapidly shoals to waist-deep water in numerous directions. As the tide has just begun to ebb, I choose not to venture through it.

I motor 'round Providence Point, the northern tip of Prudence, follow the east shore of Prudence south, and enter Potter Cove. This provides unexcelled shelter if you can tuck around the corner, excellent shelter for acres in its center, and adequate accommodation outside. The maximum depth inside is seven feet.

When I arrive, I find the cove filled with mooring buoys, most of them untenanted. There is no marina here. The remnant of a scarce-traveled road terminates at an obviously private pier. From Potter Cove, north, the island is sanctuary. To the south, numerous summerhouses peek from the woods or hover by the shore. Being overly considerate, I anchor rather than utilize one of the thirty vacant moorings. After all, it's Sunday afternoon; residents may return at any time.

Postponing supper, I paddle my kayak over to the spit of land encircling the harbor. I walk the beach on the outer side and search for unburied treasure. The shingle is various: brownstone lumps, black, non-lustrous, sedimentary slivers, granite pebbles, occasional quartz made opaque by iron oxide. The shingle is generously interspersed with thousands of common shells: Slippers and mussels predominate. Occasional bits of quahog and whelk and rock crab anoint the mixture. Random, dead horseshoe crabs and driftwood planks round out the assortment. Strands of blackened eelgrass ravel this trash together.

I pocket a few odd pebbles and shards of sea glass. One is the small square bottom of a bottle, once clear, but presently sanded opaque by the sea. The trade name SARDO is embossed across its bottom. I've since discovered that Sardo Foods began in 1965 in Sicily selling gourmet olives and olive oil, and is now headquartered in Ontario. Undoubtedly, my small square bottle once contained olive oil.

By my beached kayak stands a grove of knee-high plants with sturdy stalks. They remind me of miniature trees. The leaves resemble those of the great red oak. The fruits resemble anything but acorns. They are green and hard and elliptical, nearly hen's egg in size, but unlike most of the eggs I've known are covered in wicked spines like those of chestnuts. A hen would grow faint just contemplating any of these green eggs. One of the pods has dried and begun to split, revealing multitudinous small black seeds. These toxic plants, I later discover, are *Datura stramonium*, also known as jimsonweed or moonflower. During the summer, the long, pale trumpet-like flowers open at night to attract the moths responsible for their pollination. I leave them to propagate. Carrying one of these fruits in my blue jean pocket would not be a good idea.

Across Narragansett Bay to the east I descry the Mount Hope Bridge. It towers above small, intervening Hog Island. This suspension bridge connects the town of Portsmouth on Aquidneck Island to the mainland town of Bristol, home of the Herreshoff boats. After dark, hundreds of lights outline the bridge. Civilization, or access to it, is but four miles away.

I kayak back toward *MoonWind* in the twilight; pause to admire a gracious sloop with a clipper bow; inhale the pungent aroma of low tide; embrace the cove with both arms; reach to wear the first star on my finger.

Potter Cove

Awake to find dawn obscured by overcast, though visibility still a couple of miles. Only a handful of boats remains in Potter Cove, and only two other sailboats have occupants. Weather calls for a little wind, a little rain, and a squall of terns having breakfast on a school of baitfish outside the harbor.

But tomorrow bodes ill for a fair-weather mariner like myself: rain and rain and possible thunder squalls and numerous drops of fresh water descending all at once. I'll need to hole up somewhere all day tomorrow, and Potter Cove, though snug and lovely, is not my primary choice. The chance of precipitation waxing greater this afternoon, I pack my toys and depart. I put on my foul-weather gear over my underwear just in case, but soon take off the jacket to avoid being listed on the bill of fare as poached.

I've programmed several waypoints into my handheld GPS in case the fog rolls in or the clouds descend or night comes a half day early. But the GPS will not home in on satellites today. Mars is too close to earth this week, or the Age of Aquarius has stalled on the cusp of Reason. Whatever the cause, I have no navigation powered by electrons. As visibility seems to improve somewhat, and I have but a dozen miles to Dutch Island Harbor, I risk invoking the wrath of the gods and go.

Dutch Island is just down the way and around the bend. I carefully plot the aforesaid on my cortex and wiggle the helm. As the wind is off aiding some other sailors today, I motor the whole twelve miles, but leave my mainsail flapping to impress any motorboats I may encounter.

A massive freighter makes her way up East Passage. Behind her, the impressive Pell Bridge, connecting Jamestown to Newport, rises majestically through the haze. Her huge suspension towers nearly disappear in the low-slung sky; her mile and a half of curvaceous deck ascends two hundred feet; the catenaries of her cables swoop to perfection; at eight miles, her numerous vertical cables must be imagined.

When I've motored half that distance, I reach the foot of Prudence Island. I head due west to the farther shore of Jamestown, then follow that south. Near the head of Conanicut Island, site of Jamestown, stands a stately, antique homestead among large trees: an imposing, faded-yellow clapboard house with a large veranda, interesting roof of hips and gables, massive redbrick chimneys, stately lawns. The faded-yellow carriage house has an unusual swoop to its roof; the six-foot, fieldstone wall beside it is perforated by a row of lights below its cope. To the south there is not another house for a half mile.

I head as close to shore as I dare and wish I had a camera—not for the first time. Above me, the Jamestown Verrazzano Bridge, connected to North Kingstown, arches its back. This is the bridge I passed beneath on Friday. Another mile brings me to Dutch Island. Behind it lies a mile-long harbor, a half mile in breadth. A couple of hundred boats swing on their moorings. Stately private houses flank the Jamestown shore just above the marina, but the northernmost reach of the harbor remains conserved and undeveloped. Two hundred yards above the first house and mooring lies a marsh and long low meadows extending right across Conanicut Island, constricted here to scarcely a mile wide. It must have been two islands from time to time since its creation. Through and above this gap in the trees, the bridge to Newport looms.

I motor close to shore and drop my hook. I must make a sketch of this Pell Bridge ere I depart, though black and white will scarce convey the muted green steel, the darker trees, the silver harbor, the opalescent sky. The cables that swoop from shore to tower, tower to tower, and on again to the farther shore, begin to fade in the mist.

I go below to make a belated lunch. Suddenly *MoonWind* bumps against the bottom. There were eight feet of water where I dropped anchor and the tide was nearly out. I dash aloft and look over the side.

A seaweed-covered boulder grins hugely up at me. I haul my hook and motor a hundred yards and try again. Now I have a better perspective from which to sketch the bridge.

As I finally devour my lunch at three o'clock, a pair of loons, half changed to their winter mantles of brown and white, sport about *MoonWind.* I treat myself to coffee, recline in my cockpit, and watch these beautiful creatures enjoy the water.

DUTCH ISLAND LIGHT
NARRAGANSETT BAY
RHODE ISLAND
1857

A Caribbean 35

Woke this morning to the same glum overcast with forecast for heavy rains the entire day. As I need both potable water and ice, and have more noisome trash then my cabin requires, I tumble into my kayak at eight o'clock and paddle the calm half mile to the marina.

I tie up to the single pier just astern of a graceful fifty-foot ketch with teak decks. CAYMAN ISLANDS, it declares across her transom. As this marina has only moorings, the pier is reserved for transients and the marina's workboat and anyone who needs the use of a hose.

The harbormaster's shack has a padlocked door. I saunter up the pier with my trash and spot the ice machine, the dumpster and . . . a sailboat. She's blocked up on the shore. She has a full keel and graceful lines. A high, though tiny, center cockpit caps a lazarette stateroom and generous cabin. Massive teak railings and coamings declare her vintage. On her cabin trunk is a metal Chris-Craft logo. Just the boat I've needed: another Chris-Craft!

I wander around her and see the FOR SALE sign. A Caribbean 35, built in 1972. Only $11,500! She must be a wreck inside. I shake my head and continue to the dumpster with my trash.

"I don't need a sailboat," I tell myself. "I just need a bag of ice."

I accost the ice machine, which flaunts its shiny padlock. I glare at it in the hope of changing its mind, but this machine is used to dealing with flattery, fangless threats, and accusations. It haughtily refuses to deal with me. I go in search of someone with authority.

Two men chat in the parking lot. I stand nearby until they have done their business. One gets into his car.

"May I help you?" the other asks me.

"I need some ice," I tell him, "and your ice machine won't cooperate."

"I'll fix its wagon," he says.

He faces the machine and flourishes a small brass object. After a summary incantation, the ice chest door flies open. Some people just seem to have a knack when it comes to mechanical things.

"I saw you looking at that Chris-Craft sloop," he says.

"Who—me?" I say.

"Come on, I'll show you around her," he says. "I'm the broker."

He stands a ladder against her and up we go. Of course, she needs work. After all, she *is* a boat. Her accommodations are huge. She has more living space than most forty-footers. With a beam of eleven feet and over six feet of headroom, one could easily dance in her main salon. Her forward stateroom has a full head and shower. Her lazarette stateroom two quarter berths connected by a bench, a head with a sink, and a pair of generous port lights. Again, with six feet of headroom.

"If she were mine," the broker says, "I'd tear out those bunks in the lazarette and make a workshop back there."

"An office," I think to myself. "A library; a writing room; a den." With a laptop computer connected to the wireless network, I could work from anywhere. With a boat such as this, I could *sail* to anywhere.

Below the deck in the main salon lives a massive Perkins diesel. Generous water and fuel tanks lie elsewhere beneath the flooring.

"Her owner wants to dump her," the broker confides. "You can get her for less than he's asking."

But do I really want another middle-aged boat? Undoubtedly, she'll need to be rewired, replumbed, resanded, and revarnished. Her cockpit deck could double as a trampoline. Her hot-water heater needs replacing, her instrumentation looks quaint. Her diesel engine undoubtedly needs rebuilding. The shaft may wiggle in its bearings. Who knows what lurks between her hull and ceilings?

But she's beautiful.

And there's ample room to dance in her main salon.

Dutch Harbor

As I fill my water jug at the pier of Dutch Harbor Boat Yard, the rain begins. I quickly kayak back to *MoonWind,* nearly in time to avoid being totally melted. I use my fresh water to brew myself fresh coffee and tune in the weather forecast.

"Ten knots at *MoonWind,*" drones the announcer. "gusting to twenty. Twenty knots gusting to thirty tonight. Better move that little boat, lad. I don't like the look of those rocks."

For once I agree with him. I look at the jutting rocks by the shore, a scant hundred feet astern, and think what a rotten headache I'll have if my anchor decides to drag at two AM. I think of the boulder I met last night and wonder how many brothers and sisters he has.

I consider my options. Take out the kayak and kedge a second anchor. It's getting choppy for that. Let out my entire rode and motor to its extent and set a second anchor. Haul my anchor and motor somewhere else: perhaps pick up one of several vacant moorings nearby. Lastly: Embrace the second anchor tightly, climb with it into my nice, warm bunk, and hide beneath the covers.

I opt to move. The only danger will be when the anchor is just aweigh. I'll need to stay in gear and be ready to give it full throttle before a gust swings my bow toward shore.

It's time to take action before the wind grows worse. I don my foul-weather gear, my safety harness, my life jacket, my morion, my cuirass, my vambraces, and my greaves. I gird my trusty boat hook about my loins and go forth to win the day.

I haul my rode laboriously from the cockpit, coiling it neatly for emergency deployment. I have thirty feet of chain at the end of my rode. As soon as the chain is in my hand the bow begins to swing. I haul in another yard of chain and take two round turns with it on the nearby cleat and tend to the helm. I give her full throttle and put the helm hard over just a moment too late; the wind has pushed my bow halfway to the beach. I shove the helm hard over the opposite way, encouraging her to complete the turn.

Moon Wind slues 'round in a circle close to the shore with only a cupful of water beneath her keel. I remember the rock that she bumped just yesterday. I don't exhale until she's scrambled a hundred yards offshore. A quarter mile ahead, I capture a sturdy mooring.

I adjust its chafing gear, add more of my own, stow my rode and chain. I need to secure my anchor on deck as it tends to chafe the mooring pendant when I stow it on the bow roller. Even the heavy chafing gear on the mooring pendant may chafe through against a fluke during a roisterous night. I have no wish to test it. I go below to dry off. The increasing rain takes care of sluicing the mud from my deck. I feet so reassured and secure that I treat myself to lunch. The rain sheets down for a while and then relents. Ominous thunder comes and then departs. The sky nearly opens; then closes and glowers and weeps. I write in my journal and read and eat, then do it all again.

Tomorrow I depart to return to Noank. I haven't sailed *Moon Wind* for three days, but tomorrow there will be wind enough to spare. It's thirty-two miles by rhumb line, but the wind will blow out of the west—my destination. I may have to battle for forty or fifty miles to make it back, and the tide will ebb against me. My breakfast may grow cold before I get home. Were it not for a midday book signing the day after tomorrow I could wait for calmer weather.

It hasn't been a momentous week—so far. The weather's been fair, I've been ashore, I've played in my yellow kayak. The coffee and food and service on this yacht have been exemplary. What little entertainment there was sufficed. Although the steward was sometimes tousled he refrained from being grumpy. The choice of reading material satisfied me. The bed supported my antique back; the pillow was stuffed with down from contented geese. The radio station played my favorite music.

One of these days I'll bring the whole lot of you with me. Then the world will be peaceable once more.

Father Poseidon

Point Judith

I wake several times during the night and listen to the wind growling about Dutch Island. Daybreak finds me dazed and not very rested. I stagger up about six thirty and do my chores in order to get under way. I consider splitting a piece of hose and running it round the fluke of my plow anchor to preclude removing the anchor every time I moor. Now I rig my anchor back in the bow roller and remove my chafing gear from the mooring pendant.

The wind has died to ten knots as I cast off, but NOAA predicts ten to fifteen locally, gusting to twenty-five. Out at Block Island will be a bit rougher than Narragansett Bay: fifteen to twenty, gusting to twenty-eight. That cheers me some, though the incoming tide, abetted by a westerly breeze, shoves a four-foot chop at me as I sail toward Beavertail. The wind increases as I near the ocean. I begin to pound. It takes me four hours to make the first twelve miles.

I can only hope that the wind will blow a couple of points either way from westerly; otherwise I'll need to tack out by Block Island before I can aim for Watch Hill.

In anticipation, I've jiffy-reefed my main. At this point I have no storm jib and venture no headsail at all. If the wind proves lighter than forecast, I'll hoist my smaller genoa. I give Point Judith a generous berth before heading up to the west. I can point about 240, but have to fall off a point to climb the swells. It is now past eleven; the tide has changed and will ebb at me the entire afternoon. The wind piles up the water as I angle out toward Block Island, ten miles offshore.

After an hour, I've made scarcely any progress. As I bounce through five-footers, Point Judith Light remains two miles abeam. I start my motor. It proves rough enough that my prop comes out of the water every few moments. In order not to abuse my motor, I run it at quarter throttle.

Unfortunately, farther from shore proves even rougher. Humping over six-footers, I begin to take green water over my bow. On the nearby horizon, I can see still taller seas. Block Island disappears behind each swell.

"Well," I think. "my options are these: to prove to myself I can beat myself up some more and tack farther out; to tack closer in and hope it isn't so lumpy; to turn around and go to Cape Cod for breakfast; or to duck into Harbor of Refuge for a while, and wait till the seas abate."

This last option reeks of sanity, so I hold it in reserve. However, I come about on the opposite tack, which takes me closer toward shore. I've just passed the eastern breachway into the harbor, but I'm sure that I'll be swept past it if I attempt to enter there. If I can make another mile upwind, at least the wind and sea will carry me through the western breach in the seawall. I open my throttle another click, head up a point, and let my mainsail luff.

Conditions improve. The seas subside to mostly four-footers as I pass the Harbor of Refuge. The wind seems slightly less—about fifteen, gusting to twenty. I clip my safety harness to my mast and doused my main before it can be damaged. I can head about 290 without pounding as I climb the waves. My propeller ceases to come out of the water most of the time. I increase my throttle cautiously and shove my way into the wind at about three knots. Three knots through the water, that is. The shore scarcely perceptibly passes me by. It takes me three hours to make it past Point Judith.

My stomach, meanwhile, is far from entertained. Although I have my lunch basket in the cockpit, every time I open it, my insides begin to whimper. I keep myself amused with sips of water. The spray runs down my oilskins—some of it on the outside; my little motor whines. The sun comes out long enough to gloat and then retreats behind the sullen clouds.

I nearly doze at the helm. I stand; I sit; I even sing aloud until the seagulls scream in protest. There's only so much abuse a seagull can take.

After twenty vertical miles and two horizontal I'm past Poseidon's playground. The sea flattens out though the wind remains dead ahead. The opposing tide keeps me amply salted. I'm hungry, exhausted, and weary from pitching, but Watch Hill looms just ahead. By five o'clock, Fishers Island Sound looks good to me. Despite the mild chop that causes more spray than I've tasted all day, I know in another hour I'll be on my mooring. The tide abates; the sun burns the sea; the clouds turn a lovely purple, rimmed with gold.

I enter West Cove and hasten to my mooring. As I round up to it, thirty yards off, I lose it in the glitter. Suddenly, there it is, five yards ahead. I shift into neutral, grab my boat hook, and snag the pendant. Home at last.

BLOCK ISLAND

North Light, Block Island, New Shoreham, Rhode Island

A Business Trip

Finally able to relax with a well-deserved cup of green tea and some crackers and cheese, now that I'm on a mooring. It's nearly four o'clock and all I've had for the five-hour passage was water and an apple and a protein bar. It's tough to hang on to the tiller and cook on the stove in the galley, down below.

I got a notion about a week ago Monday that I should take advantage of this unseasonable warmth to go sailing another time before the snow flies. Of course, I knew I should feel guilty taking time off to indulge myself while the rest of the world worked, so I justified sailing by calling this a business trip. My accountant, not being a sailor, may roll his eyes.

I discovered that Block Island has two bookstores as well as a newspaper and a library. Did I tell you I decided to sail to Block Island? It's a bit over twenty miles from Noank—an easy sail when the wind is blowing. And this time of year the wind is blowing. I decided to inflict myself on Block Island. One bookstore is closed for the season; the other didn't list their email on their website. I still am old-fashioned enough to care to match a name with a smile. Not that I haven't scheduled readings via email. Not that I haven't been published in periodicals the same way. Not that I haven't had a book produced without a glimpse of my publisher.

Anyway, I prefer to shake hands with people and, afterward, look forward to their email. And it seemed that as this bookstore hadn't email, the choice came down to sailing over to see them, or calling them on the phone. And I hate phones.

So I packed my worldly goods in *MoonWind*'s lockers, as well as food for four days; studied the wind and weather on my computer; and shoved off this morning in time to ride the tide. The wind—which was moderate—blew over my shoulder. I had one reef in my main from the week before, and hanked on my smaller jib.

I'm terrible at decisions. I could have shaken out my reef, but, beyond the tip of Fishers Island, the sea seemed just a mite troubled—as though it had eaten something that disagreed with it. Like a trawler full of menhaden, perhaps, or an unwashed lobster boat. So I left that reef in, and although it never got very brisk, I made five knots across Block Island Sound.

I lay back and admired the stratified sky that tried to improve on a Maxfield Parrish painting without success. I thought about lunch. When I need to tend the helm, an apple is generally all I can easily manage. I tried running wing and wing for a couple of miles, but my roller reef prevented rigging my preventer. Yes, I should shake out that reef. I smiled at the pale sun and watched a young mermaid sporting among the waves. I'm readily distracted, this time of life. As it's difficult to watch mermaids and prevent a flying jibe, I chose to head up a couple of points and, consequently, missed the harbor entrance by a mile.

An hour from New Harbor, the wind increased; the sea kicked up; I felt justified in not having shaken out that reef in my main. I've learned you can justify nearly anything—all it requires is patience.

I rode the small rollers into the channel to Great Salt Pond, and letting my jib out the other side, surged through the harbor at five knots, wing and wing. Great Salt Pond is well over a mile long and over a half mile in width. In the summertime, you're lucky to find a spot to drop your anchor. Today a handful of boats adorned the harbor. Though most of the mooring pendants had been removed, I still had my choice of a dozen. I rounded up a hundred yards from Payne's wharf and snagged a likely mooring.

As I remarked, it's four o'clock and I've settled down to have tea. The wind is expected to yell tonight; already *MoonWind* pitches like a fractious filly. But tomorrow they promise calm. Then I can paddle ashore and ingratiate myself to the innocent town of New Shoreham. It's good to know I can treat myself to a muffin and a cup of coffee ashore and write it off as a bona fide business expense.

Overnight Frost

I didn't sleep well last night. My bunk aboard *MoonWind* wrinkled with too many memories. It dropped to freezing by dawn, and I thought my brittle ears might break each time I rolled over. When the tepid light came creeping into my cabin past my curtains, I turned away and hid in my sleeping bag. But at half past six I had urgencies of a personal nature that clamored for my attention. Being nearly awake and vertically disposed, I began my day.

I look forward to my French roast every morning. That and the chance to write down some of the facts I dream during the night. Somewhere along the way I manage breakfast. If I feel charitable I even wash my dishes. By half past nine I'm ready to face the business part of my day. This presently involved unshipping my kayak and loading her with a bag of books and flyers. As requested, the wind and sea in Great Salt Pond spread unseasonably calm. Its broad expanse lay bereft of pleasure boats this mild November.

I paddled from my mooring to the beach behind Payne's wharf, now deserted for the season. Small white jellies spangled the waters around the wharf, and feebly pulsed in the clear but cooling harbor. I ran the prow of my kayak onto the sand. The foreshore was littered with jellyfish. They reminded me of clear glass canning jar covers—the kind you affix with a bail.

I leaned my kayak against the wall that supports the end of the road. I stowed my paddles and life vest within her and tied her to a bollard.

The walk to Old Harbor—the commercial hub of Block Island—takes only fifteen minutes. I slung my sack across my shoulder and stepped forth into the future. It's a thing I do at least once a day, if only to keep in practice. The weathered cottages and the boardinghouses seemed for the most part deserted. The small salt pond beside the road had only a handful of ducks. Most of the resident populace—with and without feathers—seeks out a warmer climate for the winter.

The entire staff of the *Block Island Times* conferred how to fill their pages. They both jumped up to greet me with such alacrity that I knew they needed a story. I bestowed upon the editor a whole bookful. Then I went to the library.

The librarian was pleased to receive a book from so renowned an author. She learned I was famous—I told her so myself. She assured me the Friends of the Library would schedule a book signing for me in the summer. Anchoring in Great Salt Pond proves problematic then, but at least I won't suffer from frostbite.

One bookshop had closed for the season. The other would open at noon, a note assured me. I wandered down to Old Harbor and watched the ferry arrive. The ferry needs to back and turn to approach the landing to turn loose her cars and trucks. A brand new Peterbilt tractor-trailer nuzzled against the gate. On the starboard side, the UPS truck quietly chewed her cud. On the port side, a tousled pickup truck lowed impatiently. The skipper made a perfect landing and the deck hand raised the gate. The various vehicles bolted ashore and made their ways out to pasture.

Within the breakwater walls spreads a tiny anchorage. Of the few remaining boats, one sloop, in the shallows, rested on her bottom and leaned far over to admire her reflection. Amazing how vain some little boats can be.

I returned to the bookshop just as the clerk unlocked the door and disappeared into the back. The lights were still off as I wandered in and perused the shelves of aspiring bestsellers. The clerk, a young woman, reappeared and kindly received my journals. The owner would not return until the weekend.

By one o'clock, I'd completed all my business. With intent to frivol a bit of time, I entered a little bakeshop. I ordered a mug of homemade soup and settled at one of two tables. The sun streamed through the front window. Two pedestrians passed by the shop during the half hour I sat there. One other customer homesteaded at the far table. Johnny Cash grumbled disgruntledly from the speakers. I heard the ferry's rumbled response as she backed away from the pier.

Tomorrow I'll sail the twenty-two crisp miles home to Connecticut. I'll probably have the wind and sea to myself. For now, the afternoon is mine to enjoy. I disembark from the bakery and, stretching my arms to either shore, embrace the entire island.

The Bakery

During lunch at the bakery I talked with the woman at the only other table. As I ladled delicious pea soup into my snout, and chased the carrots cavorting in my mug, I answered her questions without distorting the truth any more than usual.

"I can spot an off-islander seven ways to Sunday," she informed me. "What are you doing out here?"

When I told her, her eyes lit up.

"My boyfriend has a thirty-foot ketch," she exclaimed. "He'd love your book."

Unfortunately, I hadn't any more with me. I gave her my card and told her to buy a few copies from my website. I remember my fantasy of sailing from harbor to harbor, peddling books. Is it that far-fetched?

I sauntered back to New Harbor. Beside the road, a Yellow Delicious apple tree, half wild, drooped above the unmown verge and dropped its imperfect fruit on the cushioning grass. Though mottled with brown, these apples evoked a life removed from the overweening presumptions of horticulture. I ought to know: I grew up with several acres of abandoned apple trees. The Yellow Delicious across our pond were stunted and hardy and tart and satisfying.

What do they do to commercial produce that makes it all so tasteless? Hopefully, when I'm dead and buried, some local worm will say to his mate, "Now *that* was a proper waterman!"

I munched an apple on my way back to Payne's wharf. I launched my kayak and explored the estuary beyond the harbor. A half mile brought me to its end. A few mallards, a few Canada geese, a clam digger and his dog, were all I met. The dog, an old black Lab, walked alongside me, shoulder-deep, to wish me a good passage. I traversed the estuary, paddled leisurely back to *MoonWind,* and secured my kayak aboard.

I made a cup of tea and wrote in my journal. The sky grew sullen; the early dusk came on; the temperature declined. I made my supper, read, and turned in early. New Harbor had scarcely a ripple. The morrow promised light air with afternoon showers.

I woke at three in the morning. The wind without New Harbor shook its antlers and stamped its hooves. *Moon Wind* had aroused to practice aerobics.

"So much for light air," I grumbled, and rolled over.

This Friday morning I tune in the National Weather Service for my morning dose of amusement. The voice on channel 1 has changed her mind.

"Ten to fifteen knots today but double that tomorrow. Better get home and sit by the fire, lad."

For once, I agree with her. By eight o'clock, I start my motor, hoist my main, and secure what needs securing. I cast off my mooring pendant, back my mainsail, and fall off the wind. Within the harbor, the breeze is a mere caress. I turn off my motor and traipse across Great Salt Pond at two to three knots. Outside the harbor, it blows about ten knots. I hank on a moderate jib and leave the reef in my main. Soon I make five knots.

The wind picks up a trifle and *Moon Wind* leans against the waters. The waist-high seas begin to break. I set a course for Wicopesset Pass at the east end of Fishers Island. I'm on a close reach the entire seventeen miles. It takes me three hours. The tide flows against me through Wicopesset as I hump my way through to Fishers Island Sound. There I need to run free against the ebb my last few miles. I slog against the chop at about two knots.

The tide sets me against the Connecticut shore. I slowly zag my way west until I can head up into the empty mooring field in West Cove. I head up, drop my rags, and start my motor. By the time I'm secure in my slip it's two o'clock. I scuff my way through the yellowed leaves into the village to Carson's, perch at the counter, and wrap my cold paws around a hot mug of coffee.

MARTHA'S VINEYARD
& THE ELIZABETHS

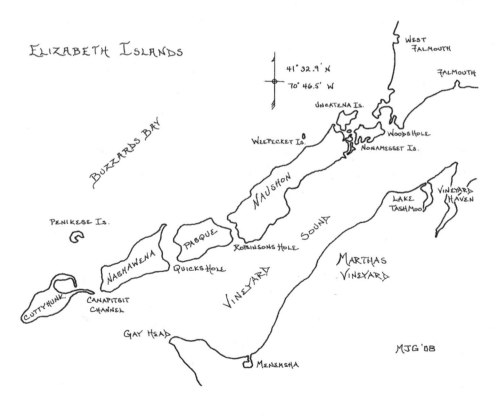

ELIZABETH ISLANDS

41° 32.9′ N
70° 46.5′ W

WEST FALMOUTH

FALMOUTH

UNCATENA Is.

BUZZARDS BAY

WEEPECKET Is.

WOODSHOLE

NONAMESSET Is.

NAUSHON

LAKE TASHMOO

VINEYARD HAVEN

PENIKESE Is.

PASQUE

ROBINSONS HOLE

VINEYARD SOUND

MARTHAS VINEYARD

NASHAWENA

QUICKSHOLE

CUTTYHUNK

CANAPITSIT CHANNEL

VINEYARD

GAY HEAD

MENEMSHA

MJG '08

224

Rain

Only a few days ere I depart for the wilds of Massachusetts. It threatens rain today but, nonetheless, I must spend this Sunday at the marina and bestow some effort on *MoonWind*. If the heavens open, in a meteorological sense, I shall have to spend the day cleaning and stowing and practicing with my GPS until I regain my familiarity with it. I still need to drive to Old Saybrook and procure a power cable.

An old friend has just called from Muenster and talked for twenty minutes. He doesn't own an automobile so he can afford to indulge his conversational whims. He reminisced about spending time on a fifty-foot chartered yawl with his parents and brothers as a boy, sailing from Southport, Connecticut to Kennebunkport, Maine. He retained an image of sailing at night; being up in the bows, stretched out on deck, and watching the moon. How can you own a boat named *MoonWind*, he asked, and not have sailed by moonlight? An appropriate question and one that I need to address.

Rain too heavy to consider doing much of anything, and more of the same predicted for Monday and Tuesday. First time in a while I haven't been at the boatyard an entire weekend—how did they manage without me?

Do I really want to be at Block Island over Labor Day weekend? No matter where I go the first couple of days, the dates won't vary. I recollect trying to anchor at Cuttyhunk over Fourth of July and having to drop our hook outside the harbor. Perhaps Point Judith Pond will be less crowded. From there, both Padenarum and Cuttyhunk are thirty miles as the black-backed seagull wings. I can sail most of the time or go ashore and mess about. After the holiday weekend, I should have little trouble finding anchorage, or space at dinghy docks. Block Island could be my penultimate destination.

Finally have charts of Buzzards Bay and the Elizabeths and Martha's Vineyard and Nantucket. If I can't find enough to do in that much area, I deserve to have Father Poseidon rend me into bait for the little flounders. The woman at the marine store said, Oh—you're headed for Buzzards Bay? How much do you draw? Powerboaters don't address one another in such a fashion. And I hadn't mentioned *MoonWind*. Only four feet, I answered. In that case, she said, you ought to check out this little harbor here [I had opened my book of charts] and this one, here. In this place you have only to pick up a mooring. Especially as you'll get there after the holiday. And in this place you can come to the pier and fill your water tank, then anchor over here and take your dinghy in to the pier and walk to the village. It isn't but a mile.

I enjoy talking to people like this. She never asked me what sort of boat I had; only my draft. I'm extra appreciative, for I'm not familiar with this part of the world and might not have hazarded going into what seem, at large scale, little more than gunk holes. Any water not having soundings on the chart needs to be entered slowly. And a mile walk will be very welcome, thank you, after a day cooped up in little boat. A mile walk any time is scarcely arduous. Every year I almost have more energy than I had the year before. Perhaps at a hundred I'll settle down a bit . . .

The rain is due to abate sometime tomorrow. Then I can complete my various projects. Firstly, to finish installing new splashboards I've made for a Lightning. Then to fit some deckhouse moldings on a thirty-eight-foot Alden Challenger. Finally, to secure my fuel tanks, inspect my chain plates, tune my rigging, refit my lazy jacks. Then, perhaps, begin to stow my gear for a two-week trip. Unless Hurricane Ernesto interferes, I should be able to cast off Saturday morning. With the wind at my back, I'll be at Point Judith well in time for supper.

Though a mile of circling breakwater shelters Harbor of Refuge, the outer harbor, it still can be an unsettled place to anchor. The seas outside the breakwater are turbulent at best. But Point Judith Pond, the inner harbor, would scarcely rock a yawning baby to sleep. The

designated anchorage is a mile behind the jetties, and the most dis-
turbance you'll likely encounter is a pair of reticent herring gulls calmly
debating the ownership of a slightly used English muffin.

Fitting Out

Nearly ready to shove off for Buzzards Bay but rain still falling as the aftermath of tropical storm Ernesto. Almost a foot of rain in Virginia and the Carolinas but scarcely enough in Noank to drown a lobster.

Worked aboard *MoonWind* yesterday and listened to the forecast. Eight- to thirteen-foot seas in Block Island Sound; twenty-five- to thirty-five-knot winds. Not a good day to venture forth in a little boat. Wind out of the northeast all day but will have veered to westerly by Monday. Tide will be ebbing all morning so shall have a free ride to Point Judith or Block Island.

Meanwhile, I trepanned the liner in the head to inspect the port chain plate that some moron had inadvisably boxed in. Why would you choose to conceal something so vital to the integrity of your vessel? I needed to know if the chain plate had been afflicted with leaks; whether the glassed-in wood was sound or whether the bolts were corroded. Everything appears sound.

Have secured my fuel tanks to eye straps and secured their covers as well. Also refastened my lazy jacks so they can be released from the boom for roller reefing. Need only replace two battens with the new ones of ash, as the ones of mahogany broke.

Went to the local marine consignment store for last-minute shopping and did quite well. Found four new spark plugs for the price of one, some hanger clips for the taffrail, and, best of all, some shelving. One of these is a magazine rack with a scroll top, made of maple but varnished. It just fit on the bulkhead above the forward settle; hopefully, I won't crack my head on its lower corner too often.

Of course, I first had to remove the bronze bell, the first-aid kit, and the dish rack. The first-aid kit went on the inside of the head door, the bell bracket to the bulkhead in the cockpit. As the bell first rings when MoonWind heels thirty-five degrees, it should prove handy. In case I fall asleep at the helm, it'll rouse me just before I wet my rail.

The dish rack barely fit abaft the aftermost port light a half step from the galley.

My other prize was a small teak rack consisting of a paper tower roller surmounted by a spice shelf. This now hangs on the outside of the head door, also only a half step from the galley. I now have paper towels within the head and without. What luxury! Eventually, the ugly plastic dispenser within will get the deep six to make way for something more elegant and useful. There's a huge space just behind the toilet, large enough to store towels. Or dirty laundry.

My magazine rack is just large enough for Mr. Richardson's chart books. The shorter front slot contains Eldridge's, repair and instruction manuals, my Coast Guard guide to aids to navigation, my little parallel rules. Also anything else I'm loath to misplace.

Now I need to stow my clothes and groceries. My toolboxes fit into brackets inside the settle lockers. In the quarter berth I've stowed my bulkier goods—hampers and bedding—to prevent their being flung about should I meet some heavy weather. Little boats are a challenge to make efficient, though single-handing allows a great deal more storage.

My stern compartment, designed for an inboard motor, holds only a twenty-gallon water tank and my battery. My single locker on the port side isn't organized at all. Some hooks for hanging cordage would be a beginning. Perhaps I'll try the marine consignment store again today.

Eventually, *MoonWind* will be an efficient little mistress; ready to reach for adventures along the coast. A trip to Maine would make a grand vacation; a visit to the Chesapeake be delightful. If only I live another hundred years, I'll get to visit every gunk hole along the eastern seaboard. And, if *you* also live another century, you'll have to endure my droll accounts of every place I've been.

Harbor of Refuge

Dropped anchor in seven feet of placid water in the lee of a woody isle of about an acre. A proper anchorage halfway up peaceful Point Judith Pond, a mile and a half above Galilee where the fishing fleet makes its home and the ferries to Block Island shuttle restlessly to and fro.

Across the narrow inlet, the villages of Jerusalem and Snug Harbor host several small marinas catering to recreational craft and a few small charter-fishing vessels. Three or four steel trawlers unobtrusively dock over here—a tenth of the ample fleet across the channel.

All this commerce defines the narrow mouth of the inner harbor. Outside the short jetties spreads the outer harbor: Harbor of Refuge: a mile-wide expanse enclosed by a seawall. Some of this wall is now in need of repair. Two generous breaches allow large ferries to meet and pass without trouble. These breaches also allow some surge to enter, but still, the outer harbor provides great refuge anytime Father Poseidon throws a tantrum.

Point Judith tends to be turbulent. When the sea is calm everywhere else, four-footers are the rule around the point. A stormy day at Point Judith has convinced any number of fishermen to take up dairy farming.

I'm telling my tale backward. Getting here, I followed the coast of Rhode Island for twenty miles past Connecticut. Off Watch Hill, I needed to blow on my sails. If it hadn't been for the running tide, I might have been there yet. Gradually, the breeze increased. Approaching Harbor of Refuge, I made five knots while surfing at a bias to the humping tide that raced to reach the seawall.

Within the refuge, I spent a half hour scouting out possible sites to drop my anchor. Even within the circling wall, the sea was not complacent. I started my motor, dropped my sails, and headed for the channel between the jetties. In twenty minutes, I rounded little Gardiner Island. This and other small islands surround the anchorage. The private houses on the mainland, a quarter mile off at either hand, stand quiet this summer evening.

Two fat, complaisant sloops raft together a hundred yards off: my only neighbors. They lean together confidingly as the glowering sky parts one last time to emit enough sun to dazzle this part of the pond. The little waters chuckle to my Whitehall tethered astern. After bouncing heavily for half the afternoon, Harbor of Refuge proved welcome, with a mere two feet of chop. By comparison, this anchorage among these tiny islands is idyllic. I can neither hear nor see the tumultuous ocean. The pond spreads calmly.

I repose in my cockpit, having a comforting coffee with cheese and crackers. My lunch, between lurches, consisted of a hard-boiled egg and an apple. I couldn't leave the helm secured for as much as a half minute once the tide and wind commenced to fling me. As I eat, a fellow in a sailboat, an O'Day 22, circles me several times to talk of boats. The three-knot breeze provides him steerageway.

Off he goes down the pond to enjoy his evening. A couple of speedboats whiz by, intent on getting to the next place in some unaccountable hurry. *MoonWind* rocks beneath me in their wake. I finish my repast and address my journal. My friend in his O'Day returns. He passes me, making nearly one knot, and heads home to his supper.

"Time to rejoin the real world," he laughs.

I'm sure the "real" world fares only too well, in its own eyes, without any aid from me. One of these days, though, I may just pay it a visit and see what all of this fuss is all about.

Whitehall and Guest

Chained to My Oars

Hanging on my hook in Point Judith Pond and taking an idle day. Idle for me. It's ten in the still, still morning and I just returned from rowing two or three miles 'round the islands. Some of the lesser ones are undeveloped. A few have solitary cottages tucked amid the trees. Others have causeways to the mainland and are thick with summerhouses.

When I slid back the hatch and poked out my nose at half past six, I startled a great blue heron perched on my Whitehall. Fortunately, my oars were secured or there's no telling where she might have gone off rowing. I was glad to see she'd controlled herself, as I haven't a shovel aboard.

Rowed across to Ram Island, which has but one cottage on it, and discovered a likely cul-de-sac half hidden in the grasses. Flushed a little blue heron; another great blue heron posed as a branch, halfway up a dead maple. Put my oars into reverse and made my way out. The next island to the north, Foddering Place, is much larger and thick with houses. Dozens of boats were moored in front but no one was messing about. Passed between the two islands and rowed down the backside of Ram. The scrubby shore supports mallow, viburnum, and stands of plumy grasses. An osprey wheeled above the pond; an angry kingfisher drove a rival out of his territory.

Rounding the bottom of Ram Island, I passed the head of Great Island, which poses as part of the mainland. Year-round houses crowd the gravelly shore. In the center of the pond, a middle-aged woman was teaching herself to sail in a pram. The force-one breeze drove her tiny sailboat at two knots. When I overtook her, we talked a bit about sailing.

"Harbor of Refuge gets rough at times," she informed me. "And the wakes that some of those big boats throw are scary. The trawlers and ferries are constantly on the go. I'm satisfied to stay right here where it's pleasant."

I continued pulling up the pond, passed *MoonWind* dreaming languidly on her anchor, and landed on Gardiner Island, fifty yards off. The shingled beach is littered with slipper shells. An acre of hardwood flanks and crowns the knoll, where trodden paths and fire pits attest to frequent use. Then I ambled the circuit of the islet, nibbling rose hips and listening to the tiny voice of the tide.

This afternoon I scull to what appears to be the head of Point Judith Pond, a mile north. A marina there caters to small powerboats, as the water runs rather shoal. But a channel before the head of the pond, with plenty of water in it, wends around a corner. Following the channel markers, I jog about a gravelly spit and find myself in a large lagoon full of deep-draft sailboats. At the head of this lagoon are two small marinas, a ship's store, a sailing school, a coffee shop, and a restaurant.

I tie off at the unused dinghy dock and enter the restaurant. There is no one about. In the empty bar, the bartender makes a pot of coffee; for me, I suppose. I take my glass mug of coffee out to the deck and stand up while I enjoy it. Walking about in the Whitehall doesn't provide sufficient exercise.

In the café, below, the employees relax, awaiting the after-work crowd. A pair of swans swims up to the nearby pier demanding food. The weekend is over; the boaters have all departed. They can't understand. The cook takes them scraps of bread and, when he returns, nurses several fingers. The swans were not gentle. The cook abuses the English language as well as the birds, describing their feeding habits.

It takes me most of a strenuous hour to fight both breeze and tide the mile and a half to *MoonWind*. Part way there, a man in a motorized rubber dinghy swerves to come alongside.

"Would you like a tow?" he inquires.

He finds it hard to believe that I choose to row. He roars away and leaves me chained to my oars.

A dozen strokes from *MoonWind*, I feel the first of many, many raindrops.

NEWPORT TOWER
NEWPORT, RHODE ISLAND

To Cuttyhunk

Rain on and off during the night. The caulking I applied last week has minimized the leak above my galley. The Weather Channel predicts a mild day. I slide my main hatch open and again surprise the great blue heron perched on my Whitehall dinghy. Perhaps I should offer her coffee.

Now programming route into GPS and soon on my way to Cuttyhunk. Harbor here just a-ripple. Overcast holds promised light above it, but air feels thick and droplets hang from my boom. I shall keep my foul-weather gear handy.

I motor the mile out of Point Judith Pond and raise my rags within the embrace of the seawall. The ebb takes me out to sea, past the tall, occulting light at the point. I flop along with the tide for a half hour, during which time the genoa coyly plays hide and seek from side to side of the mast. I drop the jib, secure the main amidships, and start the motor.

Off the mouth of Narragansett Bay, I can see the graceful leap of both the bridges in the distance: the first connecting North Kingstown to Jamestown, on Conanicut Island; the second from Jamestown to Newport, on Aquidneck Island. I see a large ketch silhouetted by the shore; another sail five miles out; one trawler and a small powerboat far astern. This nearly qualifies me as being alone.

MoonWind rises and falls on lovely soft swells, like those in my blanket in bed when I was a boy, over which my tiny toy boat would climb. Those were not so large, perhaps, but bosomy and, when I blew on my little sails, my tiny toy boat would dip in the flannel swale of the sea. *MoonWind* breasts the next swell, inhales, and glides.

Lobster pot buoys abound and I must keep my weather eye open. A quarter mile upwind steams a fishing boat. Her vivid essence is borne to me by the breeze; at a half mile it fades; at a mile, the merest redolence remains.

A larger craft appears to the east and crosses the bay swiftly. It resolves, through my binoculars, into a high-speed ferry returning from Martha's Vineyard. She certainly flies, and throws a rooster tail several feet high.

As I eat my lunch, I spy the first significant mark of my course: the red-and-white whistle off the Sakonnet River, three miles ahead. I've covered nearly half of the thirty miles. Now the breeze wakens. I slack my main and hoist my genoa. Finally turn off the motor and delight to hear the water hiss by my hull. Making only three knots but should arrive before dark. I change my course toward the south about three points.

Soon I can sight the Elizabeth Islands emerging from the haze. I scan the south with binoculars and pick out the red steel tower: Buzzards Bay light. I slant across the bay and keep a weather eye open for heavy traffic. I see but a single tow, already past me. The towrope is invisible at this distance.

The breeze is on my quarter; I make fair time. That is to say, my progress equals that of a vigorous walk. It takes the entire afternoon to cover fifteen miles. One has the expanse of Buzzards Bay to contemplate, the grace of a gull gliding grandly across the swells, the relationship of oneself to this whirling earth. One's body displaces less than a cask of brine; our Eternal Stevedore can stow billions of casks; one's mind nearly comprehends one drop of water. *Moon Wind* contemplates none of this. She lazily rolls and pushes the sea aside.

Gradually, the islands ahead transmute from nebulous blue to brown and gray and green. Now I can distinguish little Penikese Island from Cuttyhunk; I need to pass between them. Penikese has a couple of buildings that serve as a part-time school for troubled boys. It has nothing much that would qualify as a tree. I pass the red-and-green buoy at Middle Ground; spot the next red marker and then the next. It's nothing more than a nautical child's game of connect the dots.

Just without the narrow tip of Capicut Neck, I put the helm down, go forward, and dowse my jib. I drop my mainsail into the lazy jacks, start my outboard, round the light at the end of the little breakwater, and enter the natural channel to Cuttyhunk Harbor. The placid inner harbor is three parts empty. The sturdy arm of Capicut Neck surrounds this refuge, rebuffs the ragged sea. By five o'clock I'm fast to a transient mooring. A dozen other sailboats swing nearby. I secure my sails and square away my gear. I draw my Whitehall alongside and make ready to row ashore.

The village nestles against a little hill; the prospect from its summit at day's end should not be missed. The sun remains a hand's breadth up the pink and purple sky. I dip my gleaming, varnished blades into the shimmer and pull for the weathered pier at the foot of the village.

Sunset from the Summit

The piers are all but deserted. I secure my Whitehall at the dinghy dock and clamber ashore, glad to stretch my legs. In the parking lot, I talk to the fellow who runs the launch and pay him for my mooring. He's a local: one of the thirty-five folks who winter over. In the warmer months the population explodes to ten times that number. He kindly gives me the verbal tour, which I afterward confirm with eager feet.

Closer to the mouth of the harbor juts the fueling and pump-out pier. Here the New Bedford ferry has her berth. During summer, she makes two round trips per day; now but one. The Coast Guard station beside the pier has long since been abandoned.

The pier where I moor is reserved for pleasure craft; only a handful remains. The harbormaster's shack, about six by eight, stands at its head. Outside is coiled a water hose, and a bowl for any dog in need of refreshment. A sign reminds you to limit washing your vessel to ten minutes.

The third pier, close by, is commercial. A long shed over the water houses a couple of charter-fishing businesses, a lobster pound, the raw bar, and an ice cream shop. If you need ice, you can buy it from the lobster pound. Now, off-season, these businesses open at the whim of each of the owners. That is to say, about one hour, maybe, in twenty-four.

In a sturdy shed across the parking lot from my pier are two heads, but no shower. Just outside lurks a voracious telephone with an appetite for quarters. Having been taught that it's far more blessèd to receive than it is to give, this instrument devours your change and gives you lots of quietude in return.

I ask the launch driver why there aren't any showers.

"There's a limit to how much water we can provide," he says. "We

239

haven't many wells."

"Why not collect rainwater, as they do on islands in the tropics," I suggest. He smiles wryly.

"That's easily said, not easily implemented. Getting anything changed out here takes forever."

I suppose that's part of the attractiveness of an isolated island in these frenetic times. There isn't even a restaurant over here. The large B and B serves breakfast to the public during the summer, and one of the two gift shops has a bakery in it. As the baker happens also to be the postmistress, who's obliged to take mail to and from the mainland, she doesn't do much baking during the off-season, as the ferry arrives at eleven and leaves at four. During the summer, when two ferries run, she has more time between trips. Everyone out here has several jobs, or at least pursuits. One of which is to know in detail what everyone else on the island is doing.

The other gift shop keeps fresh coffee brewing. They also have the only ATM. The little market has a surprising variety. Their staff brews delicious coffee, bakes baskets of muffins, and can also make you a sandwich. In another month, they'll open their door for just one hour a day. Just up the hill stand a museum, a library, the town offices, a school that keeps two students, and one church. What more could you need?

I climb the paved road to the top of the hill that begins as you leave the harbor. Many of the houses have been set back. The verges are often unkempt with chokecherry festooned with bittersweet, inhospitable wild roses, scrubby pines, bayberry, stands of grasses and towering goldenrod, stunted sumac just starting to experiment with a wild assortment of colors. In front of some of these unkempt hedges, occasional narrow strips of lawn remain closely managed by half-tame cottontails.

The summit, though only a hundred feet high, is nearly bald, and provides unobstructed views in every direction. All two miles of Cuttyhunk descend beneath my gaze. The beryline harbor ripples below, maternally embraced by Capicut Neck. Martha's Vineyard, eight miles away to the southeast, fades hugely into a hazy blue involvement. Nashawena lies directly east, nearly as wild as before the first ship arrived. Ten miles to the north stretches the dim and reputedly civilized coast of Massachusetts. But, to the west and most of the south, uninterrupted ocean splays for miles and miles, and a regal sunset reaches pole-to-pole.

Mauve light and wisps of magenta cloud surround the settling sun. A silver dazzle harrows the cobalt sea. I dare to eye the burnished bronze star beyond, its brilliance muted. The heavens tower above me; the sea spreads a million miles. Overwhelmed, I stand on this height amid impossible beauty—and can do no more than disfigure it with words.

Exploring

I row back to the dinghy dock this morning. I first emptied my five-gallon bag and one-gallon jug into my water tank and took them with me to fill. When I get ashore, I leave them in the dinghy and take a stroll about the drowsy village.

From a side turning that smells of ripening apples, I emerge on a stretch of road fronting the beach. A hedge of beach roses is laden with huge scarlet hips and occasional shocking pink blossoms. On the inland side, cottages stand two or three deep with narrow lanes among them. Most residents utilize golf carts. At ten miles per hour in an open vehicle, you see and hear and smell everything. Stopping to talk to your neighbor is expected; exploring byways a pleasure. The parking lot by the pier is a favorite meeting place for the carting crowd; another is the market.

Carts are easily parked along the verge. A chain across the stone gateway prevents the early crowd from taking over the little porch of the market. A small, hand-lettered sign proclaims: SEPTEMBER HOURS: 8–1 AND 4–5. By next month, the hours will be reduced to 4–5. People gather and gossip outside the wall. A young woman emerges from the neighboring house, unlocks the market, turns on the red ship's light beside the door, and disappears within. A marketer takes down the chain and we file up the path.

There are bushel baskets of produce down one angle of the porch, a bench along the other. Notices pinned to the bulletin board flap in the breeze of the door. Every square foot of space within is busy. The eight of us can scarcely avoid one another. Staples and gourmet foods, snacks and household necessities crowd the shelves. You can buy a can of motor oil, a jar of capers, fresh tomatoes, or whole-grain bread. Everything has an exaggerated price. This is the cost to live on a tiny, pristine island. No one complains. I purchase a bottle of water to have the plastic bottle. I thoughtlessly brought a glass bottle and it crashes about the cockpit as I sail. It's time I hung a cup holder from my lifeline.

"Is the post office open?" I ask the girl at the counter. Not until after eleven, she informs me. That's when the ferry brings the postmistress over. The post office, just up the hill, is so small that I consider taking it with me, but the harbormaster might catch me when I load it into the Whitehall.

The library, just one size larger, keeps even scantier hours. The school next door has two small girls enrolled. The small white Methodist church proclaims that it's been in business 125 years. A couple of the citizens I've encountered here made up that first congregation.

I descend to the four corners, below the market. The door of the gift shop stands open and a woman sets out displays on the chest-high porch. I can smell fresh coffee before I reach the steps.

"Almost everything is on sale," she informs me. Summer is fleeting. I find a card made from a watercolor: *Capicut Neck in Spring Fog*.

"Oh," says the woman as she takes my money. "My cousin painted that. I see that view from my kitchen."

I stroll the two hundred yards to the piers and fill my water jugs. Then I look in at the lobster pound in search of a block of ice. Neither the proprietor nor the cat that there isn't room to swing is there. But the lobster boat lies alongside the pier and an older fellow with an earring stacks scrubbed pots on deck.

"I can sell you some ice," he says, "providin' you got the right change. They don't keep any money here."

I have the right change. He stuffs my money into a drawer and hands me a block of ice.

"Should keep pretty well," he says, "if today doesn't get too hot."

The temperature is rocketing toward seventy as I load my plunder into the Whitehall and pull away from the pier. It's already crowding ten o'clock and I plan to sail to Hadley Harbor in Woods Hole passage, fifteen miles away.

I stow the ice in my chest, restow my food, secure the cabin. The open companionway briefly frames a graceful fifty-foot cutter departing the harbor. After it passes, the companionway frames the pier where I purchased my ice; the lobster boat; the village gently ascending; the crown of the hill.

I start my motor, put the Whitehall on her tether astern, put on my life vest. Boats come and go; another island beckons. I cast off the mooring pendant and quickly return to the helm to guide *MoonWind* among her moored neighbors. I'm under way.

Bridge from Naushon to Uncatena

Hadley Harbor

Alone aboard *MoonWind,* I cast off my mooring and continue my two-week cruise among the islands off Massachusetts.

It's a warm and sunny and windless afternoon. From Cuttyhunk, I motor east up Buzzards Bay, scanning the Elizabeth Islands through my binoculars and hoping, fruitlessly, for a wisp of breeze. After a couple of hours, I'm off Naushon Island, six miles long. Rounding this will bring me into Woods Hole passage just before low water.

Hadley Harbor, my destination, lies to the west of the passage among the small islands off Goats Neck near the end of Naushon. Opposite lies Uncatena, connected by a rustic bridge. Uninhabited Bull Island shelters Hadley from the worst of the tide that tears through the Woods Hole narrows.

When I'm a mile from the green bell buoy marking the mouth of Woods Hole passage, the breeze finally arrives. I snub that breeze. I totally ignore it. I pet my motor lovingly and recount its many virtues. The breeze tries harder. No, I tell her. You had your chance three hours ago. You were off, who knows where, my lass, blowing on someone else's sails. Now you want to tempt me. I'm not about to hoist my pajamas up my mast for fifteen minutes' delight.

I motor into the passage and find the straining channel markers designating Hadley. There's hardly a house in sight. The woman in the boating store I frequent recommended Hadley Harbor.

"Just go in and pick up a mooring," she told me. "There won't be anyone there after Labor Day."

Not only is every mooring taken, but nearly every anchorage. This on the Thursday after Labor Day. Where do all these pleasure boats come from, anyway? They seem some sort of prevalent bloom that burgeons in fair weather. A couple of serious frosts will wither most of them.

The cul-de-sac behind Goats Neck has eight to ten feet of water. I drop my anchor and back down till it holds. By half past four I'm in my Whitehall pulling boat, exploring.

On Naushon, by the anchorage, is perched a diminutive boatyard with a faded, barn-red boathouse and a little tee-headed pier. At the head of this pier ride four, small, wooden, gaff-rigged Herreshoff sloops: "Twelve and a Halfs." Younger sisters of the "Petrels" that I work on at our boatyard back in Noank, they make me feel at home. Nat Herreshoff, that superlative designer of lovely craft, is alive and well among the Elizabeth Islands.

I pass beneath the picturesque miniature bridge that connects Uncatena to Naushon. Beyond spreads a shallow lagoon of a dozen acres with a noisy, roiling breachway to the sea. I row about; my blades bump on the bottom. I drift back beneath the shadowy bridge and row the other way, between Uncatena and Bull. I make a circuit of Bull Island and return through the mooring field. The squeak of my starboard oarlock rends the stillness.

Back aboard *Moon Wind,* I brew a cup of jasmine tea and sit in the cockpit, savoring both my tea and the last of the light.

Suddenly a stark white apparition, a seventy-foot long luxury cruiser, tears through the twilit anchorage toward the cul-de-sac at a nonchalant ten knots. At the ultimate moment, she backs down with roaring engines, roils the rippleless water, sedately turns, then dashes out again.

As she passes me, a boat length away, I see, in her glassed-in after lounge, a uniformed butler serve Harvey's Bristol Cream in sparkling crystal to a half dozen idle aristocrats. This is surely the way to see the harbor. No grubby little pulling boats for the likes of these proud folk.

But they never admire the sensuous moss in the shade of the bridge abutments. They never stroke the quivering flanks of lovely Herreshoff boats. They never exchange salutations with the timid brown catbird's wife in the viburnum, or have a bejeweled dragonfly light on the loom of their oar.

The apparition returns from whence it came. In the succeeding tranquility, a little bat comes by to seek her supper above the harbor.

MJG '08

Wicked Woods Hole

Off to Lake Tashmoo, west of Vineyard Haven, this afternoon. Tide will be flooding into Vineyard Sound until eleven and I ought to wait until the last hour of flood when the current should have waned. With three-foot shoals flanking a doglegged channel, I don't need a four-knot rip to shove me aground.

Just astern of me anchors a power cruiser—perhaps a thirty-five-footer. She arrived shortly after I did yesterday evening. As I watched us swing, I wondered whether my anchor might be dragging; at times there was scarcely a boat length between us. Her owner came forward on deck, talking on his mobile phone. When he finished we had a good chat. No, he didn't think I was dragging.

A fifty-foot ketch with a clipper bow, center cockpit, lazarette deck-house, her chain plates worn proudly halfway down her hull, puttered up behind him as we conversed and let go a large plow anchor trailing chain. The woman at the wheel backed her down to set it. The large blue sloop behind the cruiser called over to the ketch to say she wouldn't have room to swing at low tide as it shoaled off nearby. Heeding this advice, the woman eased the ketch forward and the man, in the eyes, winched up the hook until it cleared the water. They rounded me en route to another berth. Their anchor was festooned with eelgrass.

Anchoring in eelgrass proves problematic. If you merely toss out your hook or only set it halfheartedly, you may be only tangled in the weeds. They'll hold you for a while if it's calm, but eventually, the weeds will tear out of the bottom. One can't be too careful or have too large an anchor.

MoonWind is drenched with dew this morning but the sun will soon rectify that. When I finish washing up my breakfast dishes I'll take a short row. The slanting bridge between Naushon and Uncatena deserves a sketch.

My next destination is Lake Tashmoo on Martha's Vineyard: a non-commercial anchorage a mile's walk from the village of Vineyard Haven. My acquaintance astern informs me that a shuttle bus runs everywhere on the Vineyard. If I don't take another sponge bath soon, I doubt they'll even allow me on the bus.

After my row, I secure my worldly goods and hoist my hook. At the mouth of Hadley Harbor, the deceptive tide swirls gently. An hour before slack tide, the current should have abated through wicked Woods Hole.

"Easy as pie," I reassure myself.

"Would you like your pie à la mode?" inquires Poseidon. "We have three knots, four knots, or five knots. The five knots comes with ice cream, nuts, and a cherry."

"Well," I reply, "can I get it for here, or to go?"

"Only to go," says he, so to go I went.

Woods Hole proves entertaining. The channel markers, having had a tough night, try their best to recline to sleep it off. My outboard motor throbs its little heart out; I need all its power to control my course through the current. I race through crooked Woods Hole at nearly nine knots. The dogleg proves entertaining. The can at the corner lunges at me; it heels over and has an impressive bow wave. Its hull speed through the water is considerable, but so is its handicap. I slue by it, scarcely five yards away, and emerge at the end of the slalom course unscathed. I enter Martha's Vineyard Sound just in time to run down the Edgartown ferry.

It's only three miles to fetch the entrance to Tashmoo, but it hasn't a proper marker. There's a tiny metal light tower by the entrance; by the time you pick it up with your binoculars, you already can see the jetty. The shoals outside the entrance are deep enough for small craft but rather lumpy. In one place, it shoals down to six feet. I take a deep breath, throttle back, and tiptoe toward the jetty. Both fishermen and terns ignore me as they busily seek their dinners. I bounce through the riffles and saunter into the harbor.

Halfway up Lake Tashmoo, I drop my anchor fifty yards west of the fairway. Later, I'll wish I had taken more time to set it.

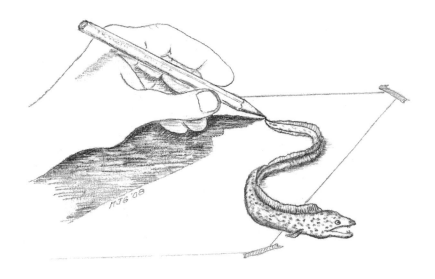

Lake Tashmoo

Yesterday, after lunch, I rowed to the town pier. This is a small, tee-headed affair. The harbormaster and the pump-out boat dock here. Dinghies, skiffs, and canoes have their own pier but also litter the shore. The tee head is for temporary use by all. A hose is available to wash the salt from your vessel or cool your coffee.

I tucked the Whitehall between two dinghies close to shore and walked to Vineyard Haven. The other name for this little town is Tisbury. Every town should have at least two names—makes it tougher for the IRS to find you.

There's quite a snug harbor in town, and a huge slip for the ferries from New Bedford and Woods Hole. The discharging and loading of cars and passengers is an event of magnitude. I imagine during the off-season there's little other amusement for the locals. Vineyard Haven is a dry town. You need to go to Edgartown or Oak Bluffs to buy your favorite libation, then go into the Black Dog Tavern in Vineyard Haven and have them decant it for you.

The transition between these two steps calls for diplomacy. In order not to offend the parched abstainers you need to conceal your bottle in a shopping bag that displays the logo of the local hardware store. Then you nonchalantly enter the tavern, whistling one of the many Temperance tunes in your repertoire. If you choose the table farthest from the door and hide behind your copy of the *Vineyard Times,* perhaps no one you know will see what you're doing and you won't have to slink home late at night by a back street. Be sure to hold your newspaper right-side up.

I decided to refrain from these diversions. There are plenty of coffee shops, and addicts of this pernicious beverage can be seen in disarray on any street, panhandling change to support their caffeine habits. One also sees children passed out from overindulgence in front of the many ice cream shops. A dissolute town, but the baked goods were exquisite.

I discovered the Vineyard Playhouse. Their theater season was over, but a blues band was scheduled for that very night at eight. I also discovered the upscale bookstore, Bunch of Grapes, where a local writer was scheduled to read from his book. A tough choice but I opted for the music. Writing is sometimes too much a part of my life.

I next discovered the small Episcopal church. In addition to having a magnificent stained-glass window depicting a dove, it also hosts a Friday-night lobster roll supper. Yesterday was Friday. As I hadn't rolled any lobsters for several months, I determined to return and revitalize my technique.

I finally walked "home" to the dinghy dock about three, to find my negligent Whitehall fast aground. The mud in Lake Tashmoo tends to be affectionate. I managed to work her free without wading in the muck, but it took me fifteen minutes. The time was well spent, however: I rediscovered a swear word that I hadn't employed in years. Back aboard, I squared away my cabin and listened to a new CD I'd purchased in the village.

By six o'clock, I was on my way back to Tisbury. I found that Episcopal lobster tastes much the same as the Congregational lobster we had growing up in my village and hardly differs from a truly agnostic lobster I martyred once before he'd taken the time to resolve his doubts.

The theater proved enchanting. On the first floor is a coffeehouse with gingham tablecloths and theater photos displayed on every wall. The theater itself, upstairs, seats perhaps two hundred. The set might have been from *The Grapes of Wrath:* the interior of a three-room shack with more lath than plaster showing. The musicians joked about it as they settled in and gave us a sweet performance. Two hours of bliss for a measly ten dollars is a bargain by any measure.

It was half past ten. The moon was full. I strolled the mile back to the pier and found the lake reposed in meditation. The muted shades of boats contrasted softly with the shadows. Impressionism must have been invented on such a night as this. The evening was delectable and I heard the mermaids calling from the harbor. I hung my boarding ladder over the side, made myself presentable, and spent the night in my cockpit cherishing hopes of being abducted.

Aground

My plan was to ride the ebb tide to Menemsha. This would begin at noon and run westerly at two knots. Menemsha, near Gay Head, has a good harbor, a pump-out, and a shower. If I don't wash my hair for another week, I'll have to go through a car wash. There's a frequent shuttle bus that serves the island. For six dollars, I can ride the bus all day.

Tropical Storm Florence is expected to pass off Cape Cod in a day or two. This decided me to head west instead of east. Nantucket is scheduled for heavy wind and steep seas.

This morning I sculled to the town pier and filled my water jug. When I returned to *MoonWind,* a domestic goose came by requesting a handout. Once you start feeding waterfowl, they become your masters. They cluster about your boat in droves demanding breakfast, supper, room service, chilled Champagne. It never ends.

I rowed to the head of Tashmoo in search of the path to the village. A gray-haired man on his sailboat directed me where to land.

"Just beach that pretty boat of yours on the lawn by the old waterworks building," he said. "If you wait a few minutes, I'll give you a ride to town."

He squared away his moored boat and got into his dinghy. Once ashore, he showed me down a path through the woods that led to a parking area. We got in his pickup truck and fell into boating talk. I neglected to mark our turning until we reached the main road. In less than a half mile he dropped me by the market and bade me farewell. I could have fared a bit better.

I bought one bagful of groceries, another full of ice, and headed home. I turned into the side road and looked for the drive that led down to the lake. Was it that one? Or maybe this? I walked up and down for fifteen minutes and encouraged the ice to melt. It gladly obliged me. By the time I noticed the waterworks building down the hill, the paper bag holding the ice had dissolved. I cradled ten pounds of dripping ice and scurried down to the water. The cold water found its way inside my shirt and explored its way down my leg.

I enjoyed a leisurely pull down the lake. In ten minutes' time, I could pick out *MoonWind,* calmly dragging her anchor. For twenty-four hours, she hadn't moved at all, but now a pleasant young breeze rippled the lake. *MoonWind* was halfway across the fairway and headed for a graceful ketch having a bright blue stripe beneath her rub rail.

"No affairs for you, my girl," said I.

It was nearly noon and time to depart. Rather than anchor again, I hastily stowed my groceries and got my motor started. By the time I was ready to get under way, we were nearly alongside the ketch. I hauled my anchor and motored out of the harbor. I secured the helm and removed the stops from my sails. Occasionally, I had to tend to the helm. I raised the main, and the breeze increased my speed. I was messing about with the jib and didn't notice where I was going. I was sailing among the moorings to one side of the channel. They were moorings for powerboats—rather small powerboats. Next thing I knew, I was fast aground in the mud.

The channel was only fifty yards off. I put the motor into neutral and quickly dropped the sails. I shifted into reverse. I churned up mud enough to thicken your chowder, but *MoonWind* squatted contentedly on the bottom. I kedged an anchor astern with the Whitehall and winched as hard as I could while revving the motor. Nothin' doin'.

The only other option was try to go forward and hope that the water was six inches deeper ahead. All I did was bury myself a bit deeper. And the tide was going out. By low tide, I'd be lying on my side. I needed to get some help while I still was buoyant. A passing boat alerted the harbormaster. I called my towing service on channel 16. They promised to have a boat there in twenty minutes. The tide continued to ebb.

The harbormaster came by in his skiff and took my line. He tried to pull me backward to no avail. When he gave up and backed his boat toward me, the slackened towline caught in my propeller and stalled my motor. It took us five minutes to get that snarl cleared.

A few minutes later, my tow service boat showed up. After trying to pull me both forward and backward, he bent a line to my halyard, backed off a hundred feet, and tipped me over until my keel broke free. I powered toward the channel, my rail awash. Success!

My little audience was greatly appreciative. I'd proved a distraction on an otherwise dull morning. If I'd had cold drinks and ice cream, I easily could have sold enough to pay my tow insurance.

Gay Head Light, Martha's Vineyard, Massachusetts

Menemsha

Out in Martha's Vineyard Sound, the wind blew at least twelve knots but gusted twenty. I was glad I had bent on the smaller of my two jibs. Off I went toward Menemsha, only nine miles away as the petrel flits. The ebb tide pushed from behind, the wind pushed from before, but the chop didn't seem severe enough to bother with foul-weather gear.

I needed to tack four times. This increased my passage to fifteen miles. Beating as close to the wind as I could, I still made five or six knots thanks to the tide. As I approached my destination, I noticed that my GPS and compass disagreed as to my actual heading. Besides, Menemsha Harbor could not be over there. I scanned the shore with binoculars. Menemsha should be in that sandy bight of shore, down there a mile. So it proved.

The sea had begun to kick up a bit; my glasses were crusting over and my hair began to stiffen. It was getting on for lunch: about four o'clock. When it gets as choppy as this, I can't leave the helm. My autopilot, the one that adapts to a tiller, still waits in its glossy catalog. I'd been in such a hurry to go aground in Lake Tashmoo that I hadn't prepared any lunch. I couldn't even pop below to snag a Yellow Delicious. The nectarine that I'd eaten at half past ten informed me that it was lonely.

"Too bad," I barked. "Get used to it. Real men don't eat lunch."

I rounded the mark at the mouth of the harbor and ducked behind the jetty. The water here was calm, the wind but a breeze. I wafted into the harbor under sail and looked about. There's a large salt pond beyond the head of Menemsha Harbor with ten feet of water in it: a perfect anchorage. I approached the head of the harbor. On a large catamaran, docked at a pier, some sailors watched my passage.

"How's the channel into the pond?" I inquired. "I draw four feet."

"Fine," they replied. "But you'll have to carry your boat."

"What?" I exclaimed.

"Just roll up your trousers," they suggested. "The channel's only knee-deep."

I found this less than amusing. When I later studied my chart for more detail, I found a note on the already diminutive insert of Menemsha. This note was printed in four-point type—I could read it with my nose squashed against the chart. Yes, the channel into the pond lacked only water. At the height of the tide, about eleven tonight, I *might* just scrape my way in. Then again, I might just go aground for the second time today.

I decided to pick up a mooring at the head of the outer harbor. There was only one problem: Some devious person had borrowed most of the water. Twenty feet from the mooring buoy, my progress suddenly halted. I quickly slacked my sails and backed off the mud with my motor. Whew! Nearly aground again. Never knew Massachusetts had so much mud.

I dropped an anchor and paid out what scope I dared. No way could I spend a night here. I called the harbormaster.

"You can't anchor there," he informed me. "Go back outside the harbor and pick up a mooring."

"Roger," I replied.

Roger is not exactly a friend of mine. More a casual acquaintance: the kind who cadges a drink, then spits on your shoe.

Outside the jetty, I spotted a likely mooring: a two-foot ball sporting a one-inch pendant. On my VHF, the weather clown brayed the worst about a tropical storm named Florence. The strident wind rattled my rigging.

Perhaps this Florence will prove a coarse, degenerate wench with an eye for reckless sailors. They say she means to lift her skirts when she reaches Georges Banks. Nantucket Sound, two hundred miles inshore from the banks, is scheduled to get twelve-footers and thirty knots;

Buzzards Bay and Vineyard Sound a bit less. The fun is due to start in earnest tomorrow. Tonight I can practice rolling out of my bunk.

So much for a sheltered anchorage and a lovely, lovely hot shower. I bounced through the chop and made a grab at the mooring. The wind swung my bow as soon as I left the helm. I missed the mooring. I motored about and made another pass at it. I managed to snag the pendant with my boat hook about amidships. Then the fun began. I got a grip on the eye splice with both hands and nearly got yanked overboard. After my arms began to start from their sockets, I had to let go. On the third attempt, the wind took me out of reach again.

The fourth attempt, I again snagged the pendant amidships. This time, I worked it inboard enough to take a half turn on a stanchion. Had I been thinking, I could have passed another line through the eye splice. I slowly worked my way forward, stanchion-to-stanchion, as *MoonWind* bucked and plunged. After several minutes, I managed to secure the line to my ten-inch forward cleat. The line barely fit through my chock. It took me several more minutes to work the chafing gear up the line and through the crowded chock.

Now that it was nearly dark, I thought I deserved some lunch. I felt disinclined to cook. Just lurching about the cabin was fun enough without falling onto a hot stove. I fixed a cold meal and rolled into my bunk with all my clothes on. If anything untoward happened, I wanted to be ready. But the wind and sea never grew that ferocious: They merely conspired to keep me awake all night. As I couldn't sleep, I amused myself by checking my mooring every couple of hours and reprimanding my dinghy, streamed astern, for wanting to ram me.

So much for riding out the blow in snug Menemsha Harbor the next two days. It made most sense to scoot across to Cuttyhunk, a mere eight miles away, during the morning lull. The tide would be in my favor. I finally dozed off about four AM. At daybreak I was up. Coffee would have to wait. The wind was only fifteen knots but I needed to head dead into it. I left my sails furled, started my motor, and cast off the mooring pendant.

By seven o'clock, I passed the mid-channel marker and entered Canapitsit Channel, which separates Cuttyhunk Island from nearby Nashaweena. By eight o'clock I was fast to a transient mooring in sheltered Cuttyhunk harbor. As the rising wind began to keen in my rigging, I cooked a delicious hot breakfast of eggs and potatoes and poured a whole pot of coffee over my head.

Back to Cuttyhunk

Now it's just past noon and the wind commences to blow. *Moon-Wind* and the other moored boats slue about. There are only a couple of dozen boats on moorings, at least half of them transients. I double my mooring line and better secure my gear. The forecast calls for gusts to thirty knots, outside. In here, we have but a foot of chop: nothing to trouble about. The wind has veered from north to northeast. Off Cape Cod, the seas are piling high.

I celebrate my arrival with a bath. I heat hot water in my kettle, climb into my tiny sink, and proceed to wash my hair. I slosh water everywhere, some of it on myself. Now that I'm clean, I can venture ashore without offending most people. At least, not by my odor.

However, I choose to spend this Sunday aboard catching up on the simple things I neglected yesterday: eating and sleeping. I read and doze and laze about and sniff the rising wind and admire the sky. The ferry makes its appointed visit and bounces against the fueling pier for half the afternoon. At four o'clock, she churns through the chop to New Bedford.

At five o'clock I'm in my cockpit having a cup of Earl Grey tea and a biscuit.

"Thank you, Radcliff. That will be all, for now."

I insert my monocle and observe a forty-foot sloop messing about the harbor. There's no other word to describe it: messing about. She's under power. A woman stands in the eyes, her boat hook ready. The man at the wheel seems to be doing little more than practicing maneuvers, perhaps getting used to a newly acquired vessel.

He approaches moorings, backs down, backs all the way to the channel, slowly turns, motors to another part of the harbor, and approaches another mooring. The woman makes no pretense of picking up mooring pendants. The skipper is in perfect control. There isn't sufficient breeze in the harbor to make his maneuvers arduous. He never exceeds one knot. Over and back for a half hour, around and around, wending among moored boats, just messing about.

Finally, his demonstration of seamanship ceases, his silent pantomime ends, he makes his exit, the lights come up, we all applaud. We lay our programs on our seats and congregate in the lobby to sip Champagne.

By sunset, the wind has died. The bright blue sky is not reflective of any incipient storm. Beneath a few dull cumulus clouds some streaks of purple spread. Our burnished star drops slowly into the sea.

During the night it is calm. Monday morning breaks bright and clear. By seven thirty, the wind whines, the darkening water ruffles. The voice on my VHF broadcasts small craft advisories with monotonous nonchalance.

"From now through Tuesday night there will be an abundance of sea serpents all about the islands. Mariners risk being eaten if they venture forth from their harbors."

Having encountered sea serpents more than once in my life, I know how wily they are. I mean to enjoy my vacation and not have to perch on a surging vessel, rail down, swinging my trusty tiller about to fend off ravenous monsters.

A couple of days at Cuttyhunk should prove a peaceful escape. If I climb about the island, I should enjoy the broad expanse of the sea without the exhilaration, it's true, of being covered with spray, but being able, instead, to wax reflective. And possibly eat some lunch without Poseidon flinging me round the cockpit.

I draw my dinghy alongside, toss my water jugs into her, and clamber aboard, bringing my lunch and binoculars. With any luck, from the far side of the island, I'll catch a glimpse of a sea serpent roiling among the breakers.

The rising wind carries me quickly to the piers.

Gosnold's Tower

Once ashore, I decide to walk to Gosnold's Tower at the west extreme of the island. Bartholomew Gosnold settled Cuttyhunk in 1602, though the settlement never persisted. The Elizabeth Islands together form the town of Gosnold, Massachusetts. In 1902 the islanders built this tower in commemoration. It is somewhat visible from sea and from the hilltop above the village but, otherwise, is rather isolated.

Beyond the village, the road despairs of paving; there is only one house, at present, out on these moors. I come to a fork in the road and take the right turning. Not the correct turning, but the right one. The road devolves to a cart track, then to a path. It wends amid salt marsh grass beside a tidal pond. The mud sucks at my sneakers and I keep to the higher verge. A dinghy and a canoe recline on their gunwales above high water beside a natural breachway. The tide tears into the pond, and I decide that I'll need at least two jumps to clear it. There is the tower before me but—no one told me it lives on its own little island. I could borrow a boat, but there aren't any oars or paddles. I return to the fork and traverse the far way around.

The left fork is dry and hard and follows the brow of the bluff above the sea. I come to outbuildings and then to the last, the only house, at this end of the island. At this season, I find it deserted. Beyond the open gate, the road is merely a grassy track. It takes me down beside the sea. A deer trail climbs among thickets and wildflowers onto an arm of land surrounding the pond. Cadaverous utility poles with antique insulators stagger beside the track. Dangling remnants of wire sway with the breeze.

I find myself nearer the tower and surrounded by old structures. A cellar hole with a leveled chimney gapes beside the path. A circular foundation, now filled with browning Queen Anne's lace, testifies to a lighthouse long defunct. Its replacement is a rusty tower bearing aloft a reflector.

At the end of the trail stands a tiny cobblestone hut. Waist-high brush grows tight against the walls. Each of the double-pitched gables has a slatted, wooden ventilator, but circulation has ceased to be a problem—the wooden roof has long since fallen in. The doorway casement records the carvings of lovers, but I can't find a date going back more than thirty years. The door has disappeared. Eight feet wide and nine feet long, the cottage hasn't a window. The pargeting inside crumbles away. Broken rafters quietly rot on the floor. Deadly nightshade creeps across the threshold.

The northeast wind attempts to rip off my jacket. The surf attacks the shore. Herds of white horses gallop down the length of Buzzards Bay. By nightfall, the horses will grow even more rambunctious. Across the bay to the north lies the dim and evasive coast of Massachusetts. Bartholomew Gosnold also stopped at what is today New Bedford, but put off settling there until the seawall could be completed.

The door and narrow windows of cobblestoned Gosnold's Tower are sealed with mortar. The tower is slim and round; its low-pitched, conical roof perches seventy feet above its tiny isle. I can't read the plaque with binoculars from a hundred feet away.

I retrace the path until I come near the shore. Everywhere are cobblestones and stranded lobster pots. I sit on a polished driftwood tree ten feet above the level of the sea. What a wave to deposit this up here! From this western point of Cuttyhunk, a mile of reef extends beneath the sea: the Sow and Pigs. Only a few rocks show themselves at high tide. Breaking seas divulge some of the others. Fishermen who know the Pigs pass through here; those who don't know them come in here but don't come out.

I saunter the drying track amid the moors. Aside from the wind, it is quiet. I see a ring-necked snake and a female catbird. Beside a broad puddle I spy the prints of a deer. A small yellow grasshopper leaps to shelter beneath the goldenrod. He and his million brothers and sisters keep this square mile of Cuttyhunk all to themselves.

Above the tide, a black-backed gull engages the twisting breeze. He swoops and slides and rises and rides for the joy of it. *MoonWind* would act in a similar fashion were I to take her out there. Bracing myself against the heave of the sea and wrestling with the tiller proves arduous at twenty knots and would be exhausting at thirty. Towing the Whitehall would soon prove hazardous. Should she surf down a wave front and catch me, she'd have the potential, being heavy, to destroy my outboard motor—or herself. If she swamped I might not be able to retrieve her. I put all thoughts of sailing aside and count the wild-flowers. The road begins to climb.

The sky is clear, the sun is bright, the fierce wind strains my sails. As I rise on the foaming crest of the road, I brace my feet, heave on the tiller, lean against the sea.

GOSNOLD'S TOWER 1902

An Island Docent

Back in the village, I find the post office open and mail my letter. I wander down to the four corners and find an elderly woman with her little brown dachshund parked in their old blue golf cart. Most people on this island favor golf carts over cars. The roads are narrow, the lanes convenient, and distances insignificant.

"Jump in," she says, "and I'll show you around the island."

"Thank you!" my feet cry gratefully. I stow my sack behind the seat and get acquainted with Queenie. She drapes herself across the seat and my lap indiscriminately. We scoot about on well-paved roads, on rutted abominations. As soon as we are clear of the "heavy traffic" in the village, she allows little Queenie to get down and run alongside.

"There's where that doe beds down most mornings," she tells me. We wait ten minutes. The doe does not appear. She restarts her buggy and we lurch around a bend.

"Folks in that grand house up there think they know about boats. Huh! Nearly wiped out the dockmaster's shack last time they made a landing."

We head back toward the beach. "That's where I find the best driftwood—right down there. C'mon, let's look. Queenie, you eat that shit, you're gonna be sick."

She has lived here for almost twenty years and seldom leaves the island. Her sister makes frequent excursions to New Bedford and keeps her supplied. She stops to talk to everyone. She offers every pedestrian a ride on the rear-facing bench in back.

It's common to see two golf carts blocking the road and their drivers exchanging news. Nothing much on this little island remains private for long.

Queenie delights in stopping to smell the flowers—and other

things less salubrious. Beach roses flourish everywhere; the hips are huge and scarlet. I pluck one to nibble and offer to pick some for my hostess.

"No," she tells me. "I can't be bothered to make any rose hip jam, but my mother always did."

In a couple of hours, we cover nearly every stretch of road except the one leading out to Gosnold's Tower. She stops at the bed and breakfast and takes some of their brochures to the ferry boat that languishes at the fueling pier till four o'clock's departure. Her skipper reclines on a bench within, a newspaper over his face. His black Lab drapes himself across the threshold and scarcely opens his starboard eye when confronted by Queenie's nine pounds of indignation. I get a guided tour of the eighty-foot boat from my companion. She leaves the brochures and we scoot back to the village.

At the boutique, I buy us each a coffee. We recline in the Adirondack chairs on the deck as Queenie cavorts with one of her many companions beneath the two apple trees beside the road.

"Coffee's good, but I gotta pee," she says. "C'mon, Queenie!"

We hurtle the two hundred yards to the public toilet by the piers. The throttle's wide open—we're making at least twelve knots. I keep one hand on my hat. She dashes up the steps to the head, Queenie hard on her heels. I admire the sky until my companion returns.

"Damn near didn't make it," she confides.

Afterward, we park in the sun but out of the wind and rest and regard the harbor. She tells me of her family. She talks of carving driftwood; of the boats she used to own. She describes her medical problems.

We spend the entire afternoon together. The market reopens from four until five. It's a major event and draws a crowd of seven. At half past three, we park outside and gossip with neighbors, that is to say, everybody, for a half hour. A passing driver stops to chat with the old fellow wearing the felt hat.

"That you I saw taking the ferry last week?"

"Thought I'd go over and visit New Be'f for a change."

"See you came back."

"Couldn't stand being around so many people."

The market opens and we all troop in. The seven of us jam the aisles. A basket of fresh-baked muffins calls from the counter. We've neither of us had lunch. After we shop, we sit in the cart and devour a muffin each.

We drive to the pier again and, after allowing Queenie to check her messages, we part. I fill my water jugs and load the Whitehall. Rowing back to my mooring against the wind is arduous: It takes me a quarter hour to row the few hundred feet. I have a fresh peach, a red pepper, and a small yogurt to add to my larder. The muffin, having received the blessing of the fleet, has been laid to rest.

I make a cup of tea and write in my journal. The wind is keening through everyone's standing rigging; the waves outside the harbor are heaping up. Florence approaches Georges Banks. Wind there gusts to fifty knots, seas run nineteen feet. Fifty miles east of here, at Nantucket, seas run a mere twelve feet. Here they are only half that. Tomorrow promises more of the same: small craft warnings are posted for fifty miles in every direction from Cuttyhunk.

But tomorrow the library opens from one till three.

Cuttyhunk Public Library

If there is magic on this planet, it is contained in water.
—Loren Eiseley, *The Immense Journey*

I suppose I could use this quote just about anywhere. Loren Eiseley, the poet and anthropologist, is one of my favorite writers: a sensitive, informed, and literate soul to whom I bonded thirty years ago.

How can I share with you all the memoirists to whom I've bonded this previous half century? Barbara Kingsolver, Paul Theroux, Henry Thoreau, E. B. White, May Sarton, Ralph Waldo Emerson, Walt Whitman, Anne Morrow Lindbergh. People who told it like it was and, hopefully, may yet be.

I could go on and on about writing and writers and my own aspirations concerning the craft and art. I've written and written but, unfortunately, the bill collector still assails my door and last time I tried to shoot him I nearly clipped a whisker off the Pusslet. Sailing off into the sunset only adds interest to my debts and, besides, the glare hurts my eyes. Nevertheless, it's proved the best choice, so far.

I meant to tell you today about Cuttyhunk Island where I spent a couple of restful days aboard *MoonWind,* while the faded small craft warning snapped and tattered.

It doesn't rain. The wind blows a bit and the seas jump up and down. The chop in this sheltered harbor proves insignificant. I decide to spend some time ashore rather than cooped in my cabin. I row to the dinghy dock, tie off my Whitehall pulling boat, and walk up the hill to the little white building alongside the tiny schoolhouse.

I discover the Cuttyhunk Public Library. Built in 1892, it hasn't grown since, though not from lack of watering, and the bookshelves threaten to burst. This time of year you find the librarians doing most of the reading. I'm looking for such prosaic things as the history of this island and Gosnold's Tower or anything else to further embellish these journals.

The two ladies who keep the library serviceable prove helpful. They do a map quest to enable me to navigate behind their formidable desk and stride the twelve feet to the far end of nonfiction.

I find what I want and then a bit more and lots of things I wasn't looking for: a book on Picasso, a book on Norman Rockwell; Modernism, Impressionism, the Masters. Everything from da Vinci to Matisse, from Klee to Oldenburg. I seem to have stumbled upon the Fine Arts section.

This is why bookshops and libraries prove more inspiring than the web. Books just jump out at you and you're forced to pause and peruse them.

I wend amid the classics of modern literature. I extract *For Whom the Bell Tolls,* and read John Donne's momentous quote from which the title is taken; reread the last ten pages. I haven't looked into this book for forty years. The weeping Maria, the resolute Pilar, the noble, shattered end of Robert Jordan.

I wander throughout the Dewey Decimal System. Some of the representative works are familiar; some appear as though they ought to be. I browse and sample, thumb some oft-thumbed pages, scan jacket reviews, read last pages first. I'm an author at large—the most reprehensible type of reader known.

I look through the children's section. They have about fifteen Oz books and a dozen Doctor Dolittles and most of the Mother West Wind Stories and millions of soothing words I haven't whispered in fifty years. I want to sit down in one of these little wooden chairs, and read and read and read until my feet don't reach the floor.

The only two children who live on this tiny island year-round have just been released from school when the library closes at three o'clock, and the two librarians, unceremoniously, pitch me out the door. One child, an attractive, dark-haired girl of nine, loiters in the schoolyard and, unaffectedly, shares her smile and bids me a soft hello.

Everyone smiles and bids one another hello here on Cuttyhunk. But Cuttyhunk is only a frivolous, backward isle in the midst of a furious sea, and a child, these days, has no right to such an innocent upbringing.

What will her world be like in fifty years?

Two Artists

I retrace my way up a driveway and behind a house undergoing renovation. This shortcut has been recommended by a woman working in her garden two doors down. Normally, I don't cut through people's yards. This house is deserted for the season and the carpenters pay no attention to me. As I return, I encounter two women behind the house, reconnoitering the way.

"Is this how we cut through to the shore road?" asks the dark-haired woman.

"Follow that driveway," I tell her, "and no matter how enticing the smell, don't get caught swiping muffins from that kitchen."

That sets them giggling, I can't imagine why. Stealing muffins on Cuttyhunk is punishable by disgrace and deportation. Later that afternoon, being chauffeured about the island by golf cart, I come across them again. They are each at an easel on opposite sides of the road. The dark-haired artist, Evening Light, is cleaning up her foldable easel and brushes with turpentine. There's evidence that she uses her flannel shirttails for a paint rag.

"I think I'll go up the road a bit and paint another picture," she decides. "The light is perfect."

My driver, the elderly woman, insists on transporting her the two hundred yards uphill. Evening Light packs up her paint box and easel and climbs aboard the cart. She perches on the rear-facing bench behind us and clings to her gear.

"Hang on tight," warns our driver.

"She has a lead foot," I confirm.

"I can't hold on," our passenger protests. "Both my hands are full."

I reach behind me and seize her peacoat collar. "Got you," I say.

"You're pulling my hair," she laughs.

"It'll grow back," I tell her.

The driver abuses her clutch and our cart springs up the hill. Were it not for my grip, Evening Light would sprawl on her face in the road. As it is, she squeals the whole half minute. Queenie gallops alongside, barking industriously. The other artist, Morning Light, waves from across the road as we hurtle by. Our driver chatters gaily. We deposit our laughing fare on the knoll. She walks about to find an inspiring prospect.

"I think you'll be better off here," I advise. "There's a marvelous view of Bermuda—look!"

Today, after leaving the library, I come across the two of them warming a bench by the harbor. They are waiting for the lobsterman to open his tiny shop. His boat is not at the pier. I impart some gossip. The lobsterman has taken his wife to the mainland to do some shopping. The pound won't open today.

We walk up hill to the market and wait outside till it opens. Another woman sits on the wall. She tells us a funny story. Earlier, a couple accosted her beside the pier.

"We have some scallops left over from last night," they informed her cheerily. "We saw how much you enjoyed them. Come by our room at five thirty and take the rest of them."

Who are these strange people, she wonders. What scallops? What room? What dinner? She shares the story with us. Morning Light explodes with laughter.

"Those are the people we dined with last night," she gasps. "They think that you are me."

There is a resemblance. The innkeeper comes by on her golf cart and hears the improbable story. "The Twins" stagger about the road, their arms around each other. They laugh so hard they need to support each other. In the midst of all this, the scallop couple drives up in their car. The two ladies approach and inflict their mirth on the innocent couple within. They are laughing so hard they can hardly recount the joke.

Meanwhile, the innkeeper and Evening Light have exchanged sandals. "The trim on hers matches my outfit," Evening Light explains to me.

As her grubby jeans and jacket are splotched with azure, vermillion, and chrome, I'm not sure just what it is she's trying to match.

The market reopens. The giggling artists bounce inside. Morning Light recalls a recipe for a spread and searches for the ingredients: peach jam, horseradish, and cream cheese. The thought of this unlikely concoction sets them off again. Giggles and snorts arise from behind the crackers. The girl behind the counter rolls her eyes.

We make our way back to the pier. The raw bar has opened. The artists purchase shrimp to share with their friends at the inn. It is time to part. The shrimp need to go on ice until supper time. We exchange hugs. Morning Light hands me a package of shrimp.

"We enjoyed your company," she says.

"You're such a free spirit, Matthew," Evening Light adds.

"You may find yourselves in a story, ladies," I warn them.

This begets more giggles. The scallop couple shows up in their car and gives them a lift to the inn. The last I hear of them is their gracious laughter.

I fill my water jugs and row out to *MoonWind*. The gale has abated. Tomorrow I'll be off to ride the wind. If it continues northeasterly, I can go to Montauk, Block Island, Point Judith, or Westport. I can possibly point as high as Padenarum, where the local boat shop makes bushels of pungent shavings, and the harbor abounds in sailboats built of wood.

For now, I remove the cutting board that covers my propane stove and put on my old black kettle and a pot of water. Ray Charles coaxes the blues from his piano as I cover the basmati rice and pare my vegetables. I stir-fry my shrimp with onion and garlic, broccoli and fresh ginger. I make a pot of green tea. My honey will just suffice to see me home.

Billie Holiday quietly croons as dusk flows over *MoonWind*. Through the companionway, the village puts on a mantle of Pointillism. The first star twinkles weakly above the island. I delay turning on my cabin lights and sit in the cockpit, savoring yet another perfect day.

The harbor has calmed considerably. The only sound is the dull thud of the sea beyond the spit. It's been a pleasant visit but the tide tugs at my spirit. Tomorrow I shall spread my wings to the breeze. I raise my mug of green tea.

Cheers, ladies! Thanks for your lovely laughter!

Across Buzzards Bay

I laze about Cuttyhunk Harbor this morning till after nine aboard *Moon Wind,* eating and scribbling. Finally under way at 0940. Outside the harbor I raise my rags, but the wind is on vacation. NOAA reports twelve knots with four-foot seas at Buzzards Bay Tower, five miles west of here. I whistle and whistle, but that breeze is hard of hearing.

I motor sail the fifteen miles across Buzzards Bay to the mouth of the Sakonnet. Here the wind picks up and backs a couple of points, enabling me to turn off my motor and claw my way across the mouth of Narragansett Bay. To clear Point Judith, I need to motor a mile dead into the wind. Then I ride the flood tide into the mile-wide Harbor of Refuge under sail, and enter the channel to Point Judith Pond with a little breeze following after. I meet the Block Island ferry heading out, but graciously avoid running her under. On the eastern jetty, generous people fling food to the fish by means of limber poles.

The wind turns weak and fitful. I start the motor, drop the jib, and step down into the cockpit just as the main decides to jibe. The boom strikes me across the temple hard enough to cure me, almost, of daydreams. I sit for a moment to compose myself, retrieve my glasses, and check the knot on my head. It hasn't a chance of winning the eggplant derby. I grab the tiller just in time to slue about the next marker.

I lower the main as I motor up the pond. The setting sun streams through narrow rents in the cloud cover. I round Gardiner Island and set my hook at dusk. My only neighbor, a thirty-two-foot Hunter sloop, rides quietly nearby. I secure and think about supper.

Queen o' Scots

This morning the pond spreads calmly. Dirty clouds begin to descend; the next two days will prove wet. The fellow in the small O'Day sloop to whom I spoke last week touted the breakfast served at Snug Harbor Marine. The mile and a half each way seems a bit of a swim. I tumble into my Whitehall pulling boat. I take my empty water jug, a towel, clean clothes, and, to propitiate the dumpster god, my favorite bag of trash.

The half-hour row both relaxes and invigorates me. Living aboard a twenty-six-foot sloop induces lethargy—except when you're rail down and bending the tiller. I look forward to a good walk following breakfast.

At Snug Harbor Marine, I tuck behind the fuel pier in the shadow of the harbormaster's shack. A stout wooden ladder, its lower rungs alive with bottom growth, ascends to the deck. Beyond the pier head crouches a squat, block building: the grocery and café. I sit at the counter along with some local fellows and stuff myself with scrambled eggs and hash browns.

The locals discuss the gastronomic propensities of striped bass. As I'm a functional illiterate in piscation, I refrain from participation in their debate. To cover my embarrassment I hide behind my corn muffin. After another coffee I'm off to see what the waterfront has to offer.

A fish market, a lobster pound, a tackle shop, a head, and a dumpster complement the café. After testing the head and worshipping briefly at the dumpster, I follow the path that leads to the next marina. This boasts a ship's store (closed), a brokerage office (ditto), the quietest engine shop I've ever encountered, and, look! Showers! Having bathed in my tiny sink the past ten days, I'm nearly ready to try something innovative.

Though normally requiring keys issued only to clients, the doors are propped wide open. The cleaning crew has just finished and they've left the bathrooms open to air and dry. I scamper back to the White-hall and row her around the piers to this marina. There's a vacant dinghy dock beside the ramp. Two fellows aboard a skiff at the pier teach their engine obscenities. The engine proves a slow learner; they need to repeat the words again and again.

"Mind if I tie up my barge?" I ask.

"Nope," says one of them, stopping to catch his breath. "You can see how busy it is. Pretty boat ya got there."

I casually sling my bag across my shoulder and nonchalantly ascend the metal gangway. There's no one about to challenge my right to be clean. I close myself in and take a long, long shower. There's more hot water than I've seen in a week and a half. I luxuriate beneath it for ten long minutes. I towel off and put on all clean clothes. Now, this is livin'!

I toss my laundry and shower kit into the Whitehall. It's time to explore. I saunter to the next boatyard where a smart-looking steel trawler rests on the ways. Noise and fume identify the welding shop. I poke my head in the door, but thirty years of working in metal shops have sated my curiosity.

Just beyond, the dried-out hulk of a wooden trawler languishes in a cradle. Her steel fasteners rust away; her planking splits; she hasn't paint enough left to cover a dinghy. Her useful days are memories of some fisherman who now spends his last years rocking on his porch in sight of the sea.

The next yard over is rather private: It's more a backyard than a boatyard. At the uttermost end of the pavement a fifty-foot, flat-top Elco motor cruiser rests on blocks and poppets.

She, too, is built all of wood. She's narrow and sleek and dynamic. Her elegant deckhouse gleams with brightwork panels, sparkles with glass. Her hull is dark blue; her vast, mahogany transom glistens with layer on layer of varnish, but there's no name blazoned across it.

A youngish man and a woman not much older are working on her. The woman comes out of the pilothouse, wiping a varnish brush, and spots me below.

"Lovely old boat," I venture.

"Built in '47," she informs me.

"Same year I was commissioned," I reply.

"I bet you're in better shape," she chuckles.

"Long as I get caulked on a regular basis," I respond.

The Elco is getting launched next week. Soon as her topsides get two more coats of blue, and her boot top stripe's renewed, and the name goes across her transom. She's heading south to be chartered by her owners.

"You mean she's not yours?" I ask.

"Don't I wish," she answers. She looks ruefully at the stiffening varnish brush.

I leave her to her fun. She's a beautiful creature. The boat, that is. Now I notice her name in gilded, Old English script across her front windows: *Queen o' Scots.*

This is the boat that belonged to our neighbors a half century ago. The husband did business with my father for many years.

When he retired, in '64, he and his lovely wife planned to take this boat from Connecticut to New Orleans via the Great Lakes. They wanted me to come with them as deckhand and cabin boy. I was seventeen. It would have been just the three of us. The trip would have taken six months. The owners were willing to fly me home from New Orleans. My father forbade me to take time off from school.

What could I not have learned on a fifty-foot boat! I'm sure my life would never have been the same. But my father had my life planned out for me. I would finish school, go to Dartmouth, as he had, get my degree in engineering, as he had, and join him in business designing and building machinery. I had little interest in designing and building machinery. I've always been a dreamer, a scribbler, a river dancer, a waterman. What would I care for machinery?

As it was, I spent twenty years running my own machine shop. I should have run away from home, but I had a wife and two children to support.

I stand looking up at the Elco, my past running through my head. I want to cry. What a beautiful boat.

Queen o' Scots stands aloof on her jack stands and disdains to notice me. After all, I spurned her when we were both in our youth and might have lived together.

Perhaps I'd have started these journals forty years sooner.

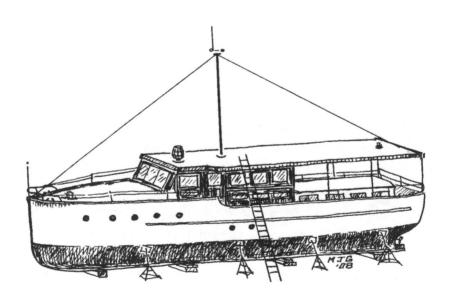

Queen o' Scots

Lethargy

I'm anchored again in Point Judith Pond, Rhode Island, aboard my old sloop, *MoonWind*. This is an estuarine pond, three miles long, connected to the Atlantic. At its mouth dock the fishing fleet and the car ferries to Block Island.

It began to rain yesterday afternoon. I returned from my excursion to Snug Harbor and battened down to count my groceries, write my memoirs, and read some of the dozen books I brought with me.

Today it rains and rains and then, for good measure, dumps water all over everything. The great blue heron, bedraggled as any fisherman can be, stands patiently in the shallows of Gardiner Island awaiting a fish. A cormorant perches on a fast-disappearing, tide-wrapped rock far out in the pond and grooms her lovely self with her fiercely hooked beak.

I've removed the uppermost drop board from my companionway and, sheltered by the overhang of the sliding hatch, peer out with my binoculars at my gray and streaming world. My Whitehall pulling boat, tethered astern, slowly fills with sweet water.

This afternoon twenty-two little sloops, a quarter mile up the pond, race 'round and 'round and 'round some marks in the rain. The open committee boat dashes about to urge or discipline them with its blatting horn. This goes on for an hour. The marks lie close together and the sailboats bunch, though many proceed in opposite directions. They remind me of water striders that skitter aimlessly on a pool.

The mouth of Point Judith Pond, a mile away, is wreathed in mist. It's another of those muted, ash and pearl and slate and jade afternoons that defy description. Had I left at the gape of dawn when the weather lulled, I might have been anchored in Great Salt Pond at Block Island, ten miles away, to watch the rain over there instead of here.

I have been away from home nearly two weeks. I am nearly out of propane. I am nearly out of coffee. I don't know which is worse. The little store adjoining the café has coffee but no propane. I may have to go ashore and gather sticks to cook my breakfast. The ice in my cooler has melted, but I've little left to keep cold.

A great lethargy has come over me. I feel reluctant to move. Tomorrow it means to clear and I should clear out. Block Island doesn't appeal to me now. On the news they tell of a whale washed up on its shore. If the weather turns warm and the breeze stays out of the south, my nose will tell me all I need to know of her demise.

Not only the weather but the lack of companionship has damped my spirit. My spiritual barometer has fallen. Two hours before the unseen sun settles behind Snug Harbor, mist and drizzle descend upon the pond. A pall enshrouds the islands; I can scarcely see my Whitehall twenty feet astern.

Talking to my journal evokes no response. My books contain but millions of dirty marks. The classical music on the radio labors lugubriously. The jazz jangles. The blues leave a bitter taste upon my tongue.

But Paula returns home soon from the isle of Rhodes in the Aegean. What tales she'll have to tell me! Three thousand years of history have swept the isles of Greece. New England's boast of four hundred years of European dominion is but a beginning. The Native Americans left few traces behind them. Though the rocks over here probably equal in age the ones in Greece, it's the art and architecture of man that arouses in me a sense of proportion, an endless quest for perfection.

The awe inspired by a cliff overhanging the sea should not be compared to the elegance of a tower or a cathedral. The natural world is stately but impersonal. Its majesty and compulsion never require our comprehension. Though the mountain crumble, yet will it outlast everyone alive. Though the ocean die of pollution, yet will it rage against the shore forever.

The Colossus at Rhodes, one of the Seven Wonders of the ancient world, stood for less than a century before an earthquake toppled it to the sea. The genius once housed by Alexandria's library swirls in the least breeze. But, despite these setbacks, we, as a race, have striven and strive and will strive all our years.

The urgency, the poignancy, the glory, the despair of civilization: All are inflicted on me by architecture and the arts. I understand the grand passion, the argument with mortality, the striving for beauty. My years diminish—my creativeness does not. I need to explore every medium; learn every craft; enshrine my soul in sculpture, artwork, words. What would *I* not attempt with these two hands, this mind, this soul?

I finish my rice and beans and wash my plate.

Block Island

Plugged in my radio last night to catch the Yankees' game and hadn't any power. The light on the inverter wouldn't light. Checked the line with my meter and found barely eleven volts. Battery is huge and only one year old and motor charges it. What's wrong?

Went aft and pushed the starter on the motor. Nothing happened. Very strange. Lights in the cabin were working—that was a blessing, though I had a lantern powered with D cells as a backup, as well as a rechargeable, million-candlepower spotlight. Maybe the power of this year's Yankees sufficed to drain my battery. Tomorrow I'll start my motor with the pull cord.

This morning I savor warmed-over rice and beans for breakfast. I need to eat them before they go bad. My ice has melted but they sat in frigid water all night and are perfectly all right. I not only haven't any ice but I've nothing to keep fresh. I'll be home day after tomorrow. I go aloft and prepare to depart. In a hopeful moment, I push the starter button. The motor starts immediately and begins to charge my battery.

Finally under way. I motor to the fuel pier at Point Judith Marina and fill my gas can and water tank. I take my trash ashore and search for a propane bottle without success. The ship's store isn't open even at ten fifteen on a Saturday morning. It's only the sixteenth of September.

Off I head to Block Island on little *MoonWind*.

Outside the Harbor of Refuge, seas are running five feet. There is almost no breeze. Close at hand, a twenty-five-foot fishing boat disappears in each trough. I flop halfway to Block Island, then start my motor. By midafternoon I power into Great Salt Pond and anchor in ten feet of water at the east side of the harbor.

I row ashore at sunset and walk the mile to the village. I order mako shark at a little restaurant. It is overcooked. I wash its dryness out of my throat with red ale. People come and go along the pavement. They strut, they slouch, they exult, they despond. They amuse me only slightly more than does the mako shark. I watch the ferry berth in the harbor before me. It discharges more people to promenade along the waterfront. I should come ashore during the day and walk. Walk away from the harbor; away from the village.

Some of Block Island is old farms. Parts of it are conserved. The twisting roads are scenic. Why do I come to the tourist part of town? The answer: to have someone cook me a meal. The trouble is, I can cook better than they can. Someday I'll learn.

I walk back to New Harbor in the twilight, light my battery lantern, and set it in the bow of my Whitehall. I pull home through the dusk. It is all but dark as I climb aboard. Did I sail out here merely to have a meal of overcooked fish?

Tomorrow I can walk about the island. I can visit both lighthouses, talk with local people. I can row about the harbor, shop for coffee and chocolate. I can buy some fish and cook a proper meal. Maybe splurge and buy a bottle of wine.

But I've done all this before.

My lethargy returns. Even the thought of going ashore depresses me. My isolation depresses me even more. I haven't any need to go ashore. I've just enough coffee for breakfast.

The next day, following breakfast, I head home.

Homeward Bound

After breakfast I hoist my anchor and get under way for Noank. The air is light from the southwest, and I make but two to three knots. If I can keep her close to the wind I can fetch the Race and take the long way home—'round the far end of Fishers Island. A part of me would prolong my trip; a part of me would be secure at the pier. I want to sail, but there hasn't been much wind since Florence ruffled the local waters. The breeze backs a bit in my favor, but when I'm halfway across Block Island Sound it dies.

I start my motor and head for Wicopesset Pass at the near end of Fishers Island: the conventional way home. I've no desire to motor any farther. Once in Fishers Island Sound, I find enough breeze to sail home the ultimate five miles. I drop my sails outside the breakwater, bring the Whitehall alongside, and putter into West Cove. I put my fenders over the side and keep my air horn ready. It's four o'clock on a Sunday, but there is almost no one about.

I round up into my slip, shift into neutral, snag my safety line from the piling, and drop it over my winch. This acts as a brake and keeps *MoonWind* from striking the walkway ahead. I hop down onto the finger pier, grab *MoonWind* by a stanchion, pull her to me, and cleat her bowline. I've returned.

I've been at large for just about two weeks. I've ranged no more than seventy miles from home as the cormorant speeds, though my log shows that I covered about 170 miles. I need more chain on my anchor rode and maybe a larger anchor. A bit more roding would make me feel more secure: I could anchor in deeper water.

A one-pound propane bottle cooks about ten meals. My four-stroke outboard, a 9.9, uses a half gallon per hour at two-thirds throttle—about five knots through the water though I average only four

knots over the ground because of tides and headwinds. I motored almost eighty miles and used ten gallons of fuel. I filled over sixty pages
in a large notebook with my scribbles—nearly fifteen thousand words.
It will take me three months—give or take five years—to expand and
edit them. I'll finish with twenty entries for fourteen days, plus two entries to describe fitting out for the trip.

I return to a dentist appointment, bills to be paid, and a pair of
lonely cats. Paula returns tomorrow.

I turn off the motor and tip it out of the water. I secure my second
bowline, my stern line, a pair of spring lines, check my chafing gear.
I coil my mainsheet and stow it. I remove my boom cover from the
locker and button it 'round the mainsail. I unhank my jib and stuff it
down the forward hatch. I coil the jib sheets and toss them down
there, too. I secure my halyards with bungee cords to the shrouds to
keep them from slapping. I snap the cover onto my bulkhead compass.

I go below and bag the jib, secure the forward hatch. I begin to
collect my belongings. Everything needn't be removed at once. The
food and dirty laundry have priority. I unstrap the spare can of gas
from the after deck and put it on the pier. I walk ashore, find a dock
cart, stack it with my belongings, and wheel it to the truck.

I return to *MoonWind,* replace her drop boards, close the hatch,
bring the hose aboard, and hose her down—anchors and hull and
deck and cabin and cockpit and motor—to remove the salt. I employ
some soap and a brush on the deck and in the cockpit. I coil the hose
and replace it on the pier. I take the heavy shore power cord from my
locker, stream it along the deck, tie it off to the bow pulpit, and plug
it in at the pier. I unscrew the waterproof cap on my deck fitting and
plug in the other end, screw down the ferrule. I turn on the switch in
the cabin and check the gauge on the battery charger.

Now I'm ready to go. I haven't cleaned the Whitehall. That can
wait till tomorrow. I run my eyes over everything, inspecting. I slide
the hatch open and reach inside to assure myself that the bilge pump
switch is set to automatic. I run my fingers down the low-voltage panel

to check that all the switches are off. I close the hatch and step down onto the pier.

MoonWind calmly bobs up and down in her slip. She'll be here for me whenever I feel the urge to sail again. Now I need to go home and tend to the Pusslets, take a hot shower, do my laundry, answer correspondence.

But now that I've returned I'm in no hurry to go ashore. I shall soon resume that rut I've worn for myself these many years. Ruts in the sea are difficult to establish. Every passage varies somewhat. Every passage one can extravagate to some degree. Every day one is driven by different breezes.

And October looms, when the wind persists and the sailing has no equal.

EPILOGUE

MJG 2011

There Was a Time

There was a time—perhaps a half century ago last Tuesday morning—when all seemed right with the world, even though I had glimmerings of what I might become. And because I was fool and idiot enough not to drown myself in the brook out back of the barn I went on to become what maybe I am today.

It was also the day that I got my first real boat. The two-oil-drum raft that I kept on the cow pond never quite, quite qualified as a really, truly boat. I mean, it floated, and it didn't tip too awfully much when I stood my sixty pounds of scrawn on any of the corners, and it never capsized completely when I shoved on my punting pole—me, Mike Fink, ascending the mighty Ohio back to Pittsburgh.

My first real boat was an eight-foot pram that resembled an Opti or a Sea Shell, except it hadn't a mast or sail or rudder or dagger board, and how would I have known what to do with all that arcane and explicit and wonderful paraphernalia, anyhow?

Now that the hair that I haven't got left is a beautiful badger gray, I've finally figured out some of what is meant to be done with some, if not all, of the gear and rigging and rags and rods that came with my current love, *MoonWind*.

You mustn't let on to *MoonWind* that I'm a novice at this sport. She's confident that I know how to sail, even when I use the unshipped tiller to fend off giggling mermaids; use the lazy jacks to hold up my trousers. Not everyone needs fifty years to discover the subtle intricacies of the boom vang. Not everyone spends months wondering what those little turning blocks by the fantail signify. The reason me and *MoonWind* get along so well is neither of us much cares that the mainsail's flying upside down. Neither of us can be bothered to count how many reefs I've taken in the keel. Neither of us is much impressed with how her anchor never drags until I go ashore.

MoonWind is much like other gals I've dated: She knows I ain't too bright, but loves me for my gaiety and my wit and my choice of coffee.

And I didn't write this to impress you with my knowledge of seamanship.

I wrote this 'cause I was pining for an innocent world when water and air and ice and sky were a part of me not prone to faded grandeur. When I traced the track of the moon upon the river with my canoe. When taxes, insurance, and mooring fees had nothing to do with rollicking upon the water, knowing oneself to be sufficient to make it home—perhaps in time for supper. It's what I intend to enjoy again before Poseidon demands I give up the helm forever and deep-six my dreams in that dreariest of havens.

So here, during a February deep, the temperature at eighteen, *MoonWind* propped up by the shore, I ponder that inevitability scarfed to the stem of this, my mortal vessel. For while I have the will to wet my keel, I would run before this world's wind to learn the creed of the wave; warm my soul at the molten sun while yet I have flesh to feel; take the helm in my willful fist while yet this arm responds. There are not many, nay, not many fair days left to the likes of me, an old waterman, to roil and glide and lean to the sensuous sea. And my joy of *MoonWind* will be my chantey all the while I scrape and paint her bottom; all the while I reeve her running rigging; all the while I stow her bushel of roding.

And when I'm away upon the wind, don't look for me on *your* calm fetch of this world.

I'll be, perhaps, in the lee of that island, yonder; be, perhaps, on the far side of that billow; be, perhaps, behind that faintest of stars that lift from the sea.

Constant Waterman

Is the nom de plume of author and illustrator Matthew Goldman. He has worked as both a toolmaker and a woodworker. He presently restores boats to support his sailing habit, and sails his sloop, *MoonWind,* to support his writing habit. He has written drama, comedy, farce, poetry, local history, boating journals, and, more recently, illustrated humorous stories for children under ninety. His numerous illustrations are available as cards and prints, and he actively seeks commissions. Please visit him on Facebook and at www.constantwaterman.com.

Constant Waterman presently resides in Mystic, Connecticut with one wife, two cats, and three boats.

VISIT CONSTANTWATERMAN.COM

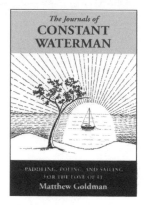

The Journals of
CONSTANT
WATERMAN

PADDLING, POLING, AND SAILING
FOR THE LOVE OF IT
Matthew Goldman

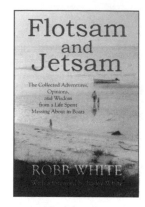

Flotsam
and
Jetsam

The Collected Adventures,
Opinions,
and Wisdom
from a Life Spent
Messing About in Boats

ROBB WHITE
With a Foreword by Bagley White

Edited by Michael Engelhard

hell's
half mile

RIVER RUNNERS' TALES OF
HILARITY AND MISADVENTURE

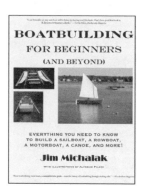

BOATBUILDING
FOR BEGINNERS
(AND BEYOND)

EVERYTHING YOU NEED TO KNOW
TO BUILD A SAILBOAT, A ROWBOAT,
A MOTORBOAT, A CANOE, AND MORE!

Jim Michalak
WITH ILLUSTRATIONS BY ALFRESH PILERO

LAPSTRAKE
CANOES

Everything You Need to Know
to Build a Light, Strong, Beautiful Boat

DAVID L. NICHOLS

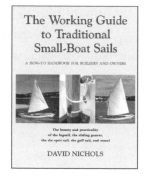

The Working Guide
to Traditional
Small-Boat Sails

A HOW-TO HANDBOOK FOR BUILDERS AND OWNERS

The beauty and practicality
of the lugsail, the sliding gunter,
the the sprit sail, the gaff sail, and more!

DAVID NICHOLS

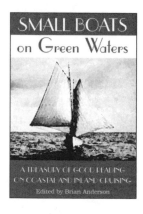

SMALL BOATS
on Green Waters

A TREASURY OF GOOD READING
ON COASTAL AND INLAND CRUISING

Edited by Brian Anderson

CHEAP
OUTBOARDS

The Beginner's Guide to
Making an Old Motor
Run Forever

Max E. Wawrzyniak III

Eye on the Sea

REFLECTIONS ON THE BOATING LIFE

MARY JANE HAYES

IN BOOKSTORES EVERYWHERE,
AND MOST ARE AVAILABLE AS E-BOOKS VIA AMAZON OR BN.COM